What About Us:

Stories of Uncontrolling Love

Edited by L. Michaels

SacraSage Press
Grasmere, ID 86753
©2019 L. Michaels

All rights reserved. No part of this book may be reproduced without consent of the author being quoted or SacraSage Press. SacraSage press provides resources that promote wisdom aligned with sacred perspectives. All rights reserved.

ISBN: 978-1-948609-17-3 (print)
ISBN: 978-1-948609-15-9 (electronic)

Printed in the United States of America

Library of Congress Cataloguing-in-Publication Data

L. Michaels Editor

What About Us: Stories of Uncontrolling Love / Michaels. Ed.

Dedicated to everyone who has a story to tell.

Contents

Introduction: How Did We Get Here? The Origin Story of this Book.....7
   L. Michaels

1. The End of the Command and Control Fathers Alliance................13
   Paul Joseph Greene

2. Tragedy, Trauma, and Triumph: Raised from the Ashes by an Uncontrolling, Loving God..35
   Mark Karris

3. The Ever-present God of Uncontrolling Love..............................63
   Janyne McConnaughey

4. Deep Calls to Deep..79
   Sharon R. Harvey

5. Essentially Uncontrolled Church...95
   Silas Krabbe

6. Is Love Enough..108
   Wendy Breningstall-Ismael

7. Friend Divorce...116
   Emma Elias

8. Don't Take Off Running...123
   Ben Graham

9. Desires of the Heart..128
   Kara Rich

10. Reconciling the God We Want to the God Who Is.....................145
    L. Michaels

11. What's Wrong and What's Right..158
    Henry Sweeney

12. The Lord Be With You: Part I..175
    Tim Reddish

13. The Lord Be With You: Part II...185
    Tim Reddish

Conclusion: Why Does Narrative Matter...194
   L. Michaels

How Did We Get Here:
The Origin Story of this Book

Asking people to share their suffering and tragedies is one of the most difficult things with which I have ever been tasked. I set out to collect stories which may have understandably caused the characters to blame God and turn away from faith but that, instead, were redeemed through the response of people who listened to and acted on God's loving persuasion to be redemptive agents in the world.

When I asked, "Would you like to be published in a book?"

The response was often initially, "Yes! Oh, yes please!"

But as the guidelines surrounding the vulnerability and risk of sharing personal experience became clearer, that answer sometimes turned to, "Oh no… No, this is not what I thought you wanted."

Introduction

And that's perfectly OK. To be fair, there were also potential participants for this project who determined that their theological commitments did not align well with the bent toward open theism and the original premise which relied heavily on embracing the concept of human free agency. That's perfectly OK, too (in fact, there was a time not so long ago when I felt the same way). The process included many ups and downs, a lot of outright rejection, and a great deal of struggling among participants (and ultimately non-participants) who questioned whether or not their stories should be told. In the end, in addition to the essays that were fully submitted for publication, there were numerous additional bits and pieces of narratives which found their ways to my inbox and my heart and which seem to indicate what I have come to know about trauma and lingering pain is true. It comes in waves and fractions of life experience that cannot always be neatly processed, shared, or integrated. It is real and raw. Even the 'completed' stories shared here sometimes end abruptly or without closure. This is intentional, because suffering is messy and the actual people who have lived these experiences are *still* living. There is no 'happily ever after' but a continual cycle of waking in the morning, falling asleep at night, and breathing in and out during the time between the two. This is often the very best we can do.

The idea for this book of essays originated as part of a domino effect beginning with Thomas Jay Oord's, *The Uncontrolling Love of God*, which gave birth to the essay book, *Uncontrolling Love*, which spiraled into a 24 hour Facebook Live event, a book tour, and countless friendships with real people who had real stories to share. There have been many moments when I have wondered how in the world I ever became a part of this! It has meant a great deal to me to engage with a community of people who are unafraid to share their lives with one another in vulnerable ways. What a privilege it has been and continues to be!

But I would imagine many people who hold this volume in their hands might wonder if these chapters are nothing more than short memoirs woven together as a public record of private events that are self-therapeutic at best and a way for the editor to make some quick cash by co-opting the narratives of a few friends, at worst.[1] I've put several years of my life into this project, in its various forms, so I sure hope this isn't the case. Instead, I would like to take a few more moments of your time, as the reader, to trace the paths that lead from theological discourse to understanding to real life action.

A substantially long excerpt from my essay in *Uncontrolling Love* reads as follows:

> *In his book,* The Uncontrolling Love of God, *Thomas Jay Oord makes a daring proposal. He has solved the problem of evil. It's a gargantuan claim yet there is much truth to this declaration. Essential kenosis presents us with an image of God that supersedes the prevalent theological debate between a god who coerces evil and a god who allows it, leaving us with a God who is fully love, unable to act unilaterally outside of this primary, defining attribute.*

---

[1] As a side note, there is no money in editing essay collections, just in case you're really wondering.

Introduction

If God is legitimately love, then God cannot be anything less. God cannot be culpable for evil, because this would contradict God's very nature, and God would then cease to be God. This shifts the blame, and the burden of culpability lands squarely on humanity, on creation, and sometimes even on random chance.

The difficult truth is, as humans we have made God into who we want God to be, and, in humility, we must admit that we have often been wrong. At this juncture, it seems like a good trade-off to shed both the controlling, hands in everything, micromanaging god and the distant, untouchable, indifferent god for the God of unending love and goodness. There is peace in this. There is comfort. When we accept that God is, indeed, lovingly doing everything God can do; we eliminate the temptation to accuse God of causing our suffering or prolonging our pain. Empathy reigns, but the problem of evil persists. People continue to experience pain, loss, and grief. This leaves me asking the question, "Now what?"[2]

Theodicy has plagued humanity, and particularly the credibility of religious communities, for the majority of human history. Why does a good God allow bad things to happen? I deeply appreciate Tom's work on this subject and I believe he brings to light an often ignored possibility which incorporates God's inability to do some things. What is more remarkable is that he paints this picture of a most-powerful God with

---

[2] Michaels, L. "Now What." *Uncontrolling Love: Essays Exploring the Love of God*, ed Chris Baker, et al. Sacrasage Press: SanDiego, CA, 2017, 315–318.

limitations in a responsible and orthodox manner! In this work, however, I am less concerned with matters of culpability and more concerned with matters of orthopraxy.

In an article responding to the horrific mass shooting tragedy of Newton, Anthony Pinn writes of a god who, perhaps, never existed and challenges humanity to stop asking the why questions, stating, "There is no justification; there is no larger logic, no theologically exposed silver lining."[3] In a later work, he posits, "To call suffering 'redemptive' or to claim it has some merit is a challenge to the integrity of human life... To the extent it can be argued that theodicy provides an answer to suffering, it does so at great risk to those who suffer most."[4] In the past, it seems as if platitudes and clichés have brought comfort to a certain subculture of people who identify as Christian, but there has never been (nor will there ever be) a legitimately sufficient answer for unspeakable suffering. As a humanist, Pinn asks questions that are similar to my own inquiries. If evil is a result of natural processes and human agency that God cannot control, then what should people be doing about it? But there is another dimension to my own thinking, and that of theologians such as Oord, which inextricably ties this human response to God's redemptive action in the world in partnership with people who desire to embody the nature of love. This culminates in a cosmic dance with multiple partners. It's not just God: It's not just us.

---

[3] Pinn, Anthony B. "God's Obituary: A Humanist Response to Mass Murder." *Religion Dispatches*, 2 Jan. 2013, religiondispatches.org/gods-obituary-a-humanist-response-to-mass-murder/.

[4] Pinn, Anthony B. "On the Question at the End of Theodicy." *Department of Religion, University of* Rice: Houston, TX, 8 Dec. 2017, 3.

Introduction

Perhaps, "God shares,"[5] until, slowly, there is a hopeful shift from the desire to understand why a good God would either create or allow such evils in the world to the desire to do something cooperatively about those same evils. Perhaps we are on the cusp of a strain of Christianity that partners with God and is moved to redemptive action in the world.

But activism alone is arguably not action, and it is also not producing measurable, fundamental change. I have a tendency toward compassion fatigue, myself. In a cultural context where media continually infiltrates our senses with short bursts of suffering and evil in the world, it is easy to become overwhelmed and to feel sad, resulting in empathetic feelings and thinking we have actually done something to alleviate the suffering, but our sadness is not embodied sympathy, because we are not, in fact, suffering in the same way (or sometimes at all).

As this began to dawn on me, I made an effort to ask people who are in the throes of suffering what I might be doing to better alleviate their intense pain. Almost without exception, the answer was, "Listen. Listen to my story."

Let's do just that...

---

[5] McFague, Sally. "Is God In Charge?" *Essentials of Christian Theology*, by William C. Placher, Westminster John Knox Press: Louisville, KY, 2003, pp. 93–116.

The End of the Command and Control Fathers Alliance
Paul Joseph Greene

Any theology of a living God and of living people should be, well, alive. And a living theology must be a loving theology. No matter how much we theologians toil to keep our theologies wrapped in impenetrable mystery, I cannot ignore the roots of a very personal quest to find the power that is compatible with genuine love. Actually, those roots of my personal theological quest are also the trunk, and the stem, and the branch, and the leaf, and the fruit.

In every class I teach, I cannot help but explore the beating heart of theology that informs an anthropology that informs a theology that informs an anthropology in rhythmic and loving pulse. So it's no surprise that in my little book, *The End of Divine Truthiness, Love Power and God*, I'm on the lookout for a wholesome theology of love and power that forms wholesome people.[1] After all, if we say people are *made in the image of God*, then everything will depend on what we mean by the word *God*. Is God a tyrant? If he is, then be on the lookout for little human imitators of supposedly divine tyranny. Is God the supreme solitary individual, aloof, needless, and disconnected from other beings? If so, brace yourself for an onslaught of hyper-individualistic narcissists. Is God love? If so, then rest assured as little human imitators bless one another with gracious hospitality and abundant generosity. That *God is love* bit is the one I like. So I'm very grateful for Thomas Jay Oord's notion of God's love as *essential kenosis as self-giving* because we live in a universe of beings whose existence depends on the mutual self-giving of all.[2] In a way it is unsurprising when the image labors to emphasize the ways her life embodies the truth of God. In fact, maybe the best way to figure out someone's genuinely held theology is to look at who they strive to be.

So, you might wonder about *this* essayist laboring away in obscurity: who does *he* strive to be? I hope you'll join me to take a look at this story of coming to be a conscientious theology professor and a better person. It is the story of the symphony of implausible causes and conditions that make my strivings possible. I am indebted beyond my imaginings to the rich

---

[1] Paul Joseph Greene, *The End of Divine Truthiness: Love Power and God* (Wipf & Stock, 2017).
[2] Thomas Jay Oord, *The Uncontrolling Love of God: An Open and Relational Account of Providence* (Downers Grove illinois: IVP Academic, 2015).

tapestry of mutually entangled existences. In retrospect, I can see in those inexhaustible causes and conditions a wisp of a thread of events that hold it all together. But, it turns out nothing could be more robust and nothing could be more resilient than that seemingly fragile thread of those entangled conditions.

It wasn't until I was 18, away from home as a college freshman, that I heard the following words from St. Benedict's *little rule book written for beginners*:[3] "hearts overflowing with the inexpressible delight of love."[4] Right away I knew exactly what Benedict meant. I knew it *from when I was a beginner*, as a little boy, from when I knew God completely. Back then God was so close there was no gap. I knew the inexpressible delight of love when, as a little three-year-old, I danced around the marshes and trees in my back yard, always accompanied, always buoyed, my heart overflowing. I knew it when I would flop onto my back in the tall grass, chewing on dandelions, the sun pouring the energy of love into my overflowing heart. I knew it when the red-winged blackbirds would call back and forth as they nested and flew around me—all our hearts overflowing. I met love in the spring muck and the summer sticky and the autumn crinkle and the winter crunch. I met the overflowing delight of love in my own nest in the bosom of a willow tree where I could chatter the overflow of love from my heart to hers. Three-year-old me knew all about powerful divine love coursing through every branch, every lung, every song, every

---

[3] Benedict of Nursia, *RB 1980: The Rule of St. Benedict in Latin and English with Notes*, ed. Timothy Fry (Collegeville, MN: Liturgical Press, 1981), 73:8.
[4] Ibid., Prologue:49.

sunbeam, every insect. And even if my personal memory of it was a little dim by age eight, eight-year-old me remembered. So when Obi Wan told us about an "energy field created by all living things [that] surrounds us and penetrates us…[and] binds the galaxy together," I knew what the old Jedi meant.[5] I knew what he called *the force* was that warm embrace, that tender companion who fills us to overflowing with love. And I was still a decade away from hearing it from St. Benedict.

Perhaps some folks will react with some dismay when I say, it frankly never dawned on me that the companion I spoke to from before I could speak had anything at all to do with church or anything at all to do with my dad who brought us to church every Sunday. The church I knew was rather barren of inexpressible delights. The church I knew certainly wasn't overflowing with love. The church I knew demanded silence from my little voice. That silence was evidently *demanded* by the *Father* I said when I tapped my forehead before tapping my tummy for the *sun* (I was very little) and my shoulders for the *spirits*. And that silence was *enforced* by my dad who slapped my hand, touched his belt, and glared me down to shut me up so everyone could pray. For a long while it kind of seemed like those fathers were just one angry person, at least until I really learned in the prayer called the "Our Father," about the Father whose will was to be done here on earth, as it is in heaven. At that point the roles of the commander Father and the controller father were clearly distinct but

---

[5] George Lucas, "Star Wars: A New Hope," (1977).

remarkably well-aligned. Really, if you tried to tell me at age four or five that the overflowing, inexpressible delight I knew had anything to do with the command and control regime of the allied Fathers, I never would have believed you.

I think my experience is a common one. Like *everyone's* life, mine was one of contrasts: terrors and delights—and everything in between. On a parallel track to my experiences of delights, in those first years of my life I also learned the meaning of terror from the enforcer-controller father. I learned the meaning of terror when I was three and called from my bed in the middle of the night to my dad's drunken abuse of my mom; when I was four and called from my bed in the middle of the night to my dad's suicidal rantings; when I was five, and my mom would go to her once a week bowling night leaving me alone with the enforcer father. I was sure the commander Father was behind all of it. Meanwhile, the delights I knew when I was sitting with the ducks, letting the rain fall on my face, being serenaded by an oriole, and napping in the willow tree could not have seemed more distant from the command and control father powers that ruled my nights and weekends.

The first brush I had with the notion that the overflowing delight of love had anything to do with church came when we moved to a new house, and a new church. It must have been Easter because my allergies were on fire from the lilies-packed sanctuary. But they smelled so great. There was something about those flowers and all the images of bunnies—so many bunnies. And baby chickens. And baby ducks. And words celebrating renewed life and second chances. Maybe it was the hymns we sang and the bright sunlight pouring into the church. It all grasped me and held me in a suspended shard of time until that afternoon when I was alone in the heat of the day: yes, it was April in Minnesota, but jeeperz it was hot, and it all flooded in at once. Love, Love, Love! Spirit, Spirit, Spirit! Sun. Sun. Sun.

Wait, S*on*! When I tap my belly it's the Son. Jesus. And it's not my belly, it's my *heart*. With a flood of inexpressible delight, it rushed into my heart. Talk about overflowing! *That's* what they're talking about at church? What? All this time? Yes. Just yes. Unbelievable. I should tell my dad; he sure needed to know. Wait. No way. No way would he get it. So, I tried to tell my Mom, 'cause I thought she might know what I meant. I must've sounded a little crazy, but she smiled. She knew, too.

Actually, it was so excellent to realize that other people knew what I had known. They just had a funny way of showing it: church. *Now, I thought, Sundays aren't so bad if we are turning our attention to that presence of love. Now,* I thought, *church isn't a regimen of enforced silence. In fact, it's chock full of words trying to express the inexpressible delight of love. Now,* I thought, *well, sure, there's plenty to sing about. Let's sing!* I started to enjoy going to church.

That vivid merging of two worlds, my visceral childhood intuition of love with the institutional response to God, gradually faded in intensity. Over the next several years, church loomed large, and my earlier experiences receded. The adult way started to replace the childhood way. But, my enthusiasm for singing in church had a funny impact on my dad. He felt some pressure to join in the singing when his son was there belting out the hymns, even though it obviously bothered him to have to sing. There is no way my dad would have even had the hymnal open if I hadn't been singing. He would sing because he was ashamed (in a cocoon of shame of his own concoction) not to be singing when I was singing.

The contrasts persisted in my home with two very different parents: a mother gifted with a passion toward empathetic love, but who, at the time, often did not have the power to make it potent; and a father who was at war with his family of origin, and who ruled our nuclear family with violence, coercion, and intimidation. All the while, we would go to church—parading in late to the front and center pew so everyone could see. And every Sunday my parents and I, and my kid sister and kid brother, listened to talk of the Father God who ruled the world as his possession through an omnipotent will and an absolute morality. The God we met at Saint John the Baptist parish was also literally male. That was made clear to me when a liberal cantor suggested changing a hymn to use more inclusive God-language, in response to which my dad raged for a week. I think we never sang that tune again. It did occur to me that if I weren't a singer, and my dad hadn't been shaming himself into singing, my dad may never have noticed the change, so I felt a little guilty about that… Anyway, every day the controller father at home imitated the commander Father we met in church. The God we met in church demanded my mom and sister *know their place* (thank God *that* didn't stick) and the enforcer Father made sure the house ran like that. The supreme owner of our house was a little enforcer father zealously imitating the divine commander, the divine bully, who enforced his will through the power of alcoholic rage.

I remember being a 7th grader struggling with math. One Saturday night of homework turned into a nightmare when my dad asked if he could help. The more I failed, the angrier he got. The angrier he got, the less clearly I could think. At last he threw me to the ground, picked me up, and pushed me against the wall so I would have nowhere to go when he whipped me with his belt for being bad at math. Then he sent me to my room to try again. My whole body tensed with terror and frustration, and the pencil snapped in my hand. When I was summoned back to report my next failure, he saw the broken pencil and knew that if *he* had broken a pencil it would have been out of defiance and spite, so he slammed me against the wall and punched me in the nose to make me bleed for those imagined offenses. Of course, I left and failed again. Repeat. I begged to stop, but this went on until he finally passed out. My mom came to my room to tend my sores and told me he did this because he loved me.

The next morning we went to church to hear stories about the Father God's beloved Son who realized he had to die and begged to stop it. But the commander Father refused the plea. The divine plan required the suffering and death of the Son. There it is. The enforcer father was living his theology. He'd been fed a steady diet of all-powerful Father God who commands the torture, abuse, and execution of his beloved Son. And it was all for love. If that's so, then what can that word, love, possibly mean? Love had become an obscene riddle.

One Sunday, when I was fourteen, a visiting priest was celebrating Mass to kick off a week of classes, worship, and overall revival (you could say) of our stodgy Catholic community. After his opening greeting, this strange priest did something I'd never seen before. He actually called me out of my pew to stand with him in the sanctuary. He had noticed my singing and was moved to publicly recognize me, call me forward, and briefly interview me. It was surreal. My heart swelled as this stranger was recognizing my obvious faith and enthusiasm. How could this stranger see my overflowing heart? He marveled when I told him my name and age: *See? A young person here with us! A fourteen-year-old with a love for Christ*, he bellowed and smiled, to boisterous applause. When the clapping trailed off, he continued, *And do you know the secret?* He paused. No one seemed to know the secret. So he would tell us. *The secret, my friends, the secret of a 14-year-old singing the opening hymn with volume, joy, and love, singing with faith and purpose*, he disclosed with great deliberate enunciation, *the secret is*— his pause gathered in every scintilla of the congregation's attention—*my friends, the secret is…*

Father power.

What, Father?

Father, *what?*

Would you stand sir? Father gestured toward my dad. My dad stood. *Look there!* Everyone looked there. *There's a father who sings the opening hymn. And look here.* Everyone looked here. *Here is a fourteen-year old who sings in church. Father power. Father power. Father power. My friends, that is the impact of Father power. Father power. Father power.*

The End of the Command and Control Fathers Alliance

While he let those words, *Father power, Father power*, pulse in a kind of slow, ludicrous chant, this strange and clueless priest tapped me on the shoulder and sent me back to the pew with the family. As I returned, the congregation clapped for my dad. They clapped for *Father power. Father power.* I think this is the day I learned the meaning of the word irony.

It was awkward in the van heading back home. We all knew the truth. And to his credit, my dad acknowledged how weird it was, after all, "if you hadn't been singing," he admitted, "I sure wouldn't have been."

I laughed, "yeah."

Even with the weird disappointment, I found the whole experience thrilling and empowering. In the coming weeks I thought more and more about how *I* could be a priest. When I become a priest, I'll be able to recognize someone with real faith, someone in touch with the inexpressible delight of love. When I become a priest, I won't make that mistake. When I become a priest, I'll be able to show people that we are totally misunderstanding the love of God. I'll be able to *see* someone who knows and shares the truth of love.

When Confirmation classes started, I thought *this is my chance* to learn all about this. I couldn't have been more excited. While I naturally dreaded algebra homework (I dreaded it even when my algebra teacher had the truly enjoyable and unfortunate name, Mr. Bader. Seriously, his name was Mister Bader), confirmation homework was always at the top of the pile. Time to learn the Apostle's Creed? *Hooray!* Time to learn about Trinity? *Hallelujah!* Time to solve for x? *Ack!* You get the idea.

So, imagine my surprise one Saturday afternoon when I was called up from my room to get the phone. I should have mentioned, this is an old timey story from when phones were attached to kitchen walls. My dad handed me the phone. It was my confirmation teacher. My heart sank the instant I heard his rumbly voice, "We missed you today at confirmation class, Paul."

I was *so mortified*. And *so embarrassed*. And so, *so, so sorry*. I'd just plain forgotten and fell all over myself with apologies and regrets. Crestfallen, I hung up the phone, turned around to face my dad and with no warning, he punched me in the nose so hard my head bounced back and knocked the phone off the hook so it fell to the floor. I was stunned. But I just stood there facing him while the blood poured out of my nose onto my shirt and onto the floor. He raged. How dare I take advantage of his home and neglect my responsibilities? Who did I think I was? What kind of twisted priorities did I have? Why won't I answer him? And now I was ruining my shirt. I should do something to stop the bloody nose. But I just stood there bleeding. I threw away the shirt.

I had just been punched, because I accidentally missed going to the confirmation class I loved to attend. I had just been punched so I would know who was in control, and it wasn't me. The allied fathers who demanded I learn, and who enforced the demand on earth as it was in heaven punched me so I would know who's boss, and so I would love Jesus. Irony grew a new dimension that day. And my enthusiasm for church was a little more muted.

The End of the Command and Control Fathers Alliance

Sure, I was confirmed. But the seamless alliance of the command and control Fathers was confirmed, too. And it turned my stomach to be seen with them in church every Sunday. When I could *finally* drive myself to church, I begged to be allowed to go to a later Mass on my own. Going alone meant I abandoned the late parade-in, so I could sit in the very back corner where no one would even notice me.

Alone with the music. Alone with the WORD. Alone with prayer.

I spent 2 years picking up the pieces. Part of my reconstruction was made possible when early on in the reconstruction the priest's homily mentioned 1 John 4:8: "God is love." I don't think it was even part of the second reading, but he must have repeated this a dozen times. So, wait? God is love? Really? That's in there? That's in the Bible? That's *always* been in there? Did *every*one know this? The command and control alliance of Fathers didn't seem to know. I *had* been right… Alone with God who *is love*, in a church full of people who now also now knew that God is love, I could feel the rekindling of the passion.

We learned from Father that day that we, the community of the church gathered, are the living presence of that divine love. We are the way God's love is put into action in everyday life. We are the way God's love shows up as compassion for someone who is hurting—the way God's love shows up as food for the hungry, clothes for the naked, companionship for the imprisoned. We, the church, are God's living presence, because we are the body of Christ. Of course this must have been preached to me before that day, but this is when I really finally heard it. What is the church? The church is the people of God doing the will of

God on earth as it is in heaven. If God wants something done, God's power works through the church. The church is the Almighty God's instrument on earth. God commands it. We do it. But, now the *it* meant *love*.

That is something I could believe in— something that I knew by heart from my childhood communion with other beings in the vast span of sunny toddler days smelling the earth and chattering with ducks. We are the body of Christ. We are the presence and effective power of love here on earth. The God who has all the power acts through us. The communal dimension of love hummed like perfect harmony in the *ear of my heart*.[6] That re-discovery primed me for yet a new surprise. Did you know that monks, who live their faith in intentional communities called monasteries, are real? I didn't.

When college, and a new Saint John's (this one in Collegeville) beckoned to me, I discovered that monasticism was actually a real thing— in central Minnesota. Astonishing. It's hard to express how flabbergasting it was to meet a community of brothers attending to the words of God *with the ear of their hearts*,[7] living so that their hearts would *overflow with the inexpressible delight of love*![8] It was like being transported to another planet— an adult version of the planet I inhabited as a little boy where the Jedi became real again. I mean, they kept weird hours, they dressed funny, but it was like there was a new Bible based entirely on the *God is love* idea. A new God. A more robust meaning for the word love.

---

[6] Benedict of Nursia, Prologue:1.
[7] Ibid.
[8] Ibid., Prologue:49.

The End of the Command and Control Fathers Alliance

When I went to church in my hometown I was always alone with a bunch of strangers, but the monastic communal life at Saint John's *called* to me. The forests and the church, the lakes and the abbey spoke to me. I remember the first time I heard Paul Simon sing about *Olodumare smiling in heaven*, and I was pretty sure that meant heavenly Saint John's.[9] Sure, there were bunches of people called Father—and they were priests. But there were also brothers! No need to be ordained. No need to become a Father. You could be just a *brother*! And I thought, maybe, just maybe, I had a future there as Brother Paul. Actually I was convinced. Here it was. People utterly devoted to nothing except their role as the body of Christ; devoted to nothing except being the presence of God on earth, doing the will of God on earth as it is in heaven. And their *Rule* knew what I knew *about hearts overflowing with the inexpressible delight of love*. Brother Paul. Yes. In this place where the beauty of nature with its lakes and songbirds and deer and forests and prairies and ducks was merged with the beauty of the community of God making God's will alive on earth— here I could find a new family, a new family where the allied fathers of command and control were not in residence… or so I thought.

Of course, it turns out, it wasn't a new planet. When one by one my life was beset by stories of friends and loved ones abused by priests and monks, things started to feel eerily familiar. When the Abbott started to give victims, people close to my heart, copies from law books implying they had no legal case against the Abbey, there was that old reliable

---

[9] Paul Simon, *Lyrics 1964-2008*, 1st Simon & Schuster hardcover ed. (New York: Simon & Schuster, 2008), 224.

command and control Father alliance. They *were* in residence. When the preaching at Mass didn't square up with the maltreatment of friends, there it was again: the command and control regime back for another run. Somehow, the insidious, demented old theology that empowers the powerful to harm vulnerable people was alive and well even at my beloved Saint John's.

Monastic life receded into impossibility. Senior year barreled toward me. Alas, in my youthful religious certainty, I had abandoned majoring in Spanish and secondary education—and the possibility of gainful employment—in favor of English and theology, fields of study that confronted me with the dreadful reality that I was prepared to do, well, not much of anything, except maybe be a novice monk… I was beyond lucky to land an internship teaching theology to 10th graders at the Prep School on campus and also lucky a monastic friend agreed to oversee my student teaching. Who could have guessed that hastily arranged experience, in the midst of the wreckage, would ignite my love of teaching? But it did.

Senior year brought more wreckage: the final dissolution of my parents' marriage. After 25 years of physical and emotional abuse at the hands of the enforcer husband, my mom filed for divorce. The strains and pressures of my dad rescinding his promise to pay for my education meant I dropped down to one meal per day as I fumbled through student teaching and my final courses to complete my BA. My little sister saved me when she bought me groceries. The strains and pressures of the separation and the selling of the family house tore at the fabric of our family, and my siblings and I were required to pick sides. For me, it was easy to oppose the command and control alliance of Fathers, as my family of origin splintered, and my monastic family of choice disintegrated.

Through it all, my mom showed some remarkable strength, which she drew from her Catholic faith—the faith she adopted when she left her Lutheran upbringing to be able to marry my dad. It seemed astonishing: Could the same faith that propelled the abuse of the father alliance also be the faith that strengthens resolve to break free from that command and control regime? My mom kept going to church. My mom kept making hot dishes for funerals. My mom kept praying. The riddle of the same religion bolstering both sides was bewildering, but the punch line was devastating. When word got around to folks at church that my mom was divorcing her husband, everything changed. The priest told her to stop coming to communion. Seriously. Stop coming to communion for having the strength to leave a man who beat her up and beat up her kids? Can you *imagine*?

That did it.

So, you're telling me, God has all the power, and the church is the body of Christ enacting the will of God on earth as it is in heaven—and *this* is what God does? God *bulldozes* my friends who are victims of clergy sexual abuse? God refuses communion to my mom because she is not willing to submit herself and her children to further abuses? The instrument of God, the church as the body of Christ that enforces the will of God on earth is siding with the abusers? If that is true, then the meaning of the phrase *God is love* is just plain absurd. The final straw came in the hypocrisy that made a mockery of love. At the time I was trapped in the idea that the Almighty God has a will that cannot be thwarted—because (in truly dizzying fashion) the wielder of all the power *of course* gets what he wants. When that was linked with my wholehearted acceptance of the idea that the church does the will of that God, I had to conclude that God was the author of the abuse. Disgusting.

Though Dr. Sam Harris hadn't written these words yet, I was face to face with the truth behind them: "At the heart of every totalitarian enterprise one sees outlandish dogmas, poorly arranged, but working ineluctably like gears in some ludicrous instrument of death."[10] The totalitarian enterprise of the command and control regime of the fathers alliance could not be fixed by a veneer of what Dr. Martin Luther King Jr. calls *anemic, sentimental, and powerless love.*[11] Even worse, how could I love, or pray to, let alone *worship* a God whose love is abuse? I couldn't. So, by 1998, with so many friends abused by clergy and my own mom excluded from communion, I was done with all of it. Done with church. Done with God. Done with religion. And done, done, done with the abusive command and control alliance of Fathers.

Then something weird happened on a Saturday morning. We were a few years into nineteen years of remodeling a 1911 duplex (yeah: slowest flip ever), when I ran up to the attic to grab a hammer. The TV had been left on (okay, I did it) and the anchor, Frank Vascellero was speaking

---

[10] Sam Harris, *The End of Faith: Religion, Terror, and the Future of Reason* (New York: W.W. Norton & Company, Inc., 2005), 101.

[11] Martin Luther King Jr., ""Where Do We Go from Here?," Delivered at the 11th Annual Sclc Convention," kinginstitute.stanford.edu, https://kinginstitute.stanford.edu/king-papers/documents/where-do-we-go-here-delivered-11th-annual-sclc-convention (accessed January 9, 2017).

The End of the Command and Control Fathers Alliance

during a segment in the fluffy Saturday morning news show. He said that on Monday at 8 am there would be a karaoke contest at the ticket counter of Northwest Airlines (Northwest Airlines is something that used to exist—ask your parents). I almost didn't hear the next bit, but I paused when he said the word "prize." What could I win? Frank said I could win five round trip business class tickets to anywhere in Asia Northwest Airlines flew. There was some charming newsroom banter about how clever it is to have a karaoke contest to publicize their new non-stop flights to Osaka, Japan. But all I could think is, *my sister is adopted from South Korea—and she's never been back. Three of us could go there. And there'd still be one more trip for two!* So I thought, *By gosh by golly I'm doing this.* And *I'm going to win. What does Northwest Airlines want? They want a spectacle for this publicity*—so I went dressed up like Elton John, sang an Elton tune, and made it onto the evening local newscasts. And I won. No joke.

The additional tickets meant a chance to go to Thailand, where I was surprised to meet so many Buddhists. I'd never met a Buddhist. Not that I could recall, anyway. But, in Thailand *every*one was Buddhist. The temples were everywhere: beautiful, sensational with sights and sounds and smells that captured my spirit. Here were so many lovely Buddhist people living a life of seamless integrity across all parts of life. I thought, *this is my chance!* I can be a spiritual person again with no talk of God and Fathers, and no talk of church. Here in the warm embrace of the Buddha I could let my spirit expand again, but not under the surveillance of the command and control Fathers alliance. The Buddhism books I brought back with me ignited my mind no less than my spirit, and it wasn't long before I'd found Thich Nhat Hanh's books *Living Buddha, Living Christ*[12] and the brand new *Going Home: Jesus and Buddha as Brothers*.[13] At first the titles shocked me, but before I knew it, I was sneaking off at lunch to noon Mass at the Basilica of St. Mary with my Thich Nhat Hanh books hidden under my arm!

How could that have happened? What could that possibly mean? To figure out how learning about the Buddha's dharma could propel me back to church, I decided to earn a master's degree in theology. My master's thesis, "The Sevenfold Sacrament of Generous Interbeing," was a Buddhist-Christian dialogue to help me understand how this happened. The penultimate step toward my master's degree was to submit my thesis. That day, my advisor told me he'd finally figured out what I had constructed in my Buddhist-Christian dialogue—a particular kind of theology I'd never heard of: process theology. In fact, he told me with great enthusiasm, I really needed to read Whitehead, Cobb, Gilkey, Haught, Teilhard de Chardin… I had to stop him. All I could say was, *Whoa! No way! Thank you very much, but I'm done.*

Well, turns out he was right. I was wrong. I wasn't done. I did have to read those authors. So, a few years later I got my PhD to explore this whole new (well, new to me) kind of theology of the ongoing process of divine open and relational love. Imagine my delight to read that

---

[12] Thích Nhât Hanh, *Living Buddha, Living Christ* (New York: Riverhead Books, 1995).
[13] Thích Nhât Hanh, *Going Home: Jesus and Buddha as Brothers* (New York City: Riverhead Books, 2000).

according to the philosophy of organism by Alfred North Whitehead the imperial God was "the most natural, obvious, idolatrous theistic symbolism."[14] Well, duh! Nothing was more obvious to me. But how wonderful to finally discover that there were other people who also knew it.

Now, how did this happen? How did I get here? Because I ran upstairs to get a hammer? And then I said yes. And yes again. And again. Actually, so many people said so many yeses to support and love me. In this journey since running upstairs to grab that hammer, I've encountered a very new open and relational way to understand how God works in the world, how God works in real human lives. Actually, in another sense, I've just been re-connected with the experience of love I knew as a little kid.

The divine love creates new opportunities for new life in places where there appears to be no way—as Monica Coleman says, God works by *making a way out of no way*.[15] The divine love is less about control and requirement, and more about a persuasion and call. As Oord says, "because God must act like God, God must love," and that means "uncontrolling love… comes first in God."[16] *Uncontrolling love* is the invitation to each new moment, pregnant with new possibilities, for

---

[14] Alfred North Whitehead, David Ray Griffin, and Donald W. Sherburne, *Process and Reality: An Essay in Cosmology*, Corrected ed., Gifford Lectures 1927-28 (New York: Free Press, 1929), 343.

[15] Monica A. Coleman, *Making a Way out of No Way: A Womanist Theology*, Innovations: African American Religious Thought (Minneapolis, MN: Fortress Press, 2008).

[16] Oord, 161.

anyone willing to say *yes*. This is a God who provides by revealing Godself in the bosom of the willow, sci-fi movies about the Force, the drear of church, the fumblings of visiting priests, suffering monastic communities, thoughtful thesis advisors, the lessons of irony, philosophers of organism, and TVs I probably shouldn't have left on when I was out of the room. There is a wisdom in this entangled world that is the divine love, urging us in each new moment to *step toward new freedoms* and a better existence.[17]

Actually, the *narrative of the relational entanglements* is so vast that it cannot be written. And they are all the children of the God whose love is vast, open, and relational as well. Actually, my life is awash in vast giftedness and breathtaking generosities to which my own feeble gratitude blushes with inadequacy. The tangled up workings of love are strong and persistent, effective, and ineradicable. But, beyond any doubt, the strength of divine love does not function through some command and control regime in the alliance of the Fathers. The power of God does not control the world, or shield us from sufferings, yet it exceeds comprehension and is best known in "the tender elements in the world, which slowly and in quietness operate by love."[18] That re-discovery about the real nature of powerful divine love makes it possible for me to work as a theologian, a teacher, and a writer. And every day it makes me want to be a better person. So, yeah. God is love. Really. That's in there. That's in the Bible. And, best of all—it's true.

---

[17] Thích Nhât Hanh, *Stepping into Freedom: An Introduction to Buddhist Monastic Training* (Berkeley, Calif.: Parallax Press, 1997).
[18] Whitehead, Griffin, and Sherburne, *Process and Reality: An Essay in Cosmology*, 343.

The End of the Command and Control Fathers Alliance

Paul Joseph Greene has lived his entire life in Minnesota, so he regularly crushes on lakes and lakey sunsets and lakey twilights—and then he posts the pictures he took with his phone. In spite of the occasional demoralizing April blizzard, Minnesota means home, and family, and love. He is the author of The End of Divine Truthiness: Love, Power, and God—*a book with a similar heartbeat to Thomas Jay Oord's* The Uncontrolling Love of God—*but with an interfaith twist and a splash of Stephen Colbert's jaunty satire. You should totally check it out. Sure, Paul went into oodles of debt for a pile of degrees in English, systematic theology, and monastic spirituality. But, it was all worth it because he is lucky enough to make a living doing what he loves, teaching as an assistant professor of theology at St. Kate's in the Land of 10,000 Lakes (well, of course there are more than that, but we don't like to brag)— and a quadrillion or so mosquitoes (well, of course there are more than that, but...).*

www.pauljosephgreene.org

@PaulJGreene

facebook.com/DrPaulJosephGreene

Tragedy, Trauma, and Triumph: Raised from the Ashes by an Uncontrolling, Loving God[1]
Mark Karris

The food prepared by our mom came out of the oven and was thrown violently down on the kitchen floor by my father. Then our mother, furious with rage, quickly found a large knife in the kitchen drawer. They began yelling and cursing at each other. The venom of their callous words began to poison their all-ready bruised hearts. They saw see each other as the enemy. Little did they know that their perpetual wars would wound innocent bystanders for the rest of their lives.

---

[1] Adapted from material previously published in Mark Karris, *Season of Heartbreak: Healing for the Heart, Brain, and Soul* (Grand Rapids: Kregel, 2017).

Tragedy, Trauma, and Triumph

Our mom told us to quickly go outside. My two brothers and I anxiously ran out the front door. It wasn't the time to question. We knew it was simply time to obey. We heard what seemed like two angry monsters engaging in an epic battle. My brothers and I looked at each other but remained silent with shock and disbelief. We were scared. We didn't know what was going to happen. Then our mother, wielding that fierce knife chased our dad out of the house. I was six when that happened. That was one of the only memories I remember of my mother and father being together; if you can call that "being together." Unfortunately, that was not the only traumatic event that I experienced in my life.

In this essay, or rather story, I share with you the many snapshots of mini-stories of tragedy and trauma that have affected me to my core. They are stories involving divorce, drug addiction, abuse, mental illness, murder, depression, suicidal tendencies, a religious cult, shame, and fear. However, they are not only stories involving loss and pain; they are stories that encompass resilience, hope, love, and gratitude. The thread of redemption and healing qualities in my life is due to the ferocious, uncontrolling, others-empowering, self-giving, incredible love of God; both through God directly and indirectly through those who funnel His love through their lives.

As a licensed therapist, ordained pastor, and theologian, I will interweave psychological insights and theological tidbits throughout these stories. I will also share invaluable life-lessons I learned in the aftermath of trauma, healing, and helping others. My hope is two-fold. It is to help me remember and remind myself of what I have learned along this wild ride of dis/organized chaos we call life. My hope is to also benefit you, the reader, as you walk through your own spiritual path toward ever-increasing experiences of shalom.

Divorce: The Great Divide

As you can guess, my parents divorced after the infamous knife wielding incident. The odds were quite stacked against them anyways. They had twins when they were eighteen (I am one of them). A year later they had my younger brother. That makes three kids at nineteen. I guess they lasted six years together, which was remarkable considering the circumstances. But, they divorced. And it certainly was not a friendly one. There deep love for one another quickly turned into a tenacious hatred. Unfortunately, the greatest casualties of warring parents are usually the children.

While my brothers have had their own perspectives on our past, I can only sure mine. I am not sure what I thought when I was six. I didn't have an adult brain so it certainly was not integrated thoughts. I do remember fear being the predominant emotion. I remember being divided. Whose side was I supposed to be on? Who was I supposed to love more? What do I do with my dad picking us up on the weekend and calling my mother every name under the book? What do I do with my mom periodically keeping us from our dad, just to spite him? I was afraid. I was confused. I felt divided. I had to shut down and hide my emotions. I had to placate whichever parent I was with. The loss of potential love was too great to risk being congruent.

Not only was I divided within myself but there became an even greater barrier between my parents and me. Their hate for one another blinded them, keeping them from seeing me as an innocent child who was in need. I was desperate for affection and for them to compassionately listen to my hurting heart. But, instead of them seeing me as a person, I was just a projection for them to throw their verbal vomit at. Their focus on hurting the other diminished the already little presence they were able to offer previously.

Shame, Pain, and Growing Up Lame

Sure, everyone's family is dysfunctional. Even Adam and Eve, the first set of parents, had a child who killed his brother. And, I am also sure most people's adolescent years were difficult. For me, my parents took dysfunction to a whole other level. And the adolescent years were like walking through a minefield blindfolded.

A few years after my parents divorced, there were guys in and out of my mom's house. I didn't know who was coming or going. It is hard to forget this one guy though. When I was sick, he gave me dog flea and tick shampoo. Sure, it was probably a drug-induced accident but boy did I spend school that day sick as a dog (pun intended). I almost made it through the day until I projectile vomited on the bus drive back home. After some time, one-day I came home and there was an almost 6-foot tall, heavily tattooed, 300-pound, biker guy sitting on the couch. "Who was is this scary intruder?" I thought to myself. He would eventually become my step-dad.

Mark Karris

My mom and step-dad were well-known drug dealers in the neighborhood. Yes, they both did drugs too. Actually, my mom was addicted to drugs as far back as I can remember. I can't imagine how many second-hand highs I experienced growing up. The living room was like a continual cloud-fest filled with either cigarette smoke or THC, the euphoric compound in marijuana that gives people their high. With drugs also came violence, not only outside of the home, but inside the home.

There are no words that I can use to express the fear and rage I had as a kid growing up in my mother's house. To hear the weekly earthquakes in the home and the smacking and pounding of flesh, knowing it was full-well my mother getting beat, are not sounds any child should hear. Sure, my mom was pretty fierce. I am sure she didn't go down easily. But she was no match for the giant who was my step-dad. One day, at around twelve years old, I had enough. Adrenalin filled me like high-octane jet fuel. I went out of my room, got into between them both, looked up at the angry giant, gritted my small teeth and screamed, "Don't you touch my mom anymore!" "Smack!" Instantly, I fell to the ground in utter defeat. It turned out I was also no match for him.

At some point, my brothers and I went to live with my father. We must have been thirteen or so. My dad worked seven-days a week. He certainly provided us a place to live and made sure there was food on the table. Unfortunately, he did not know how to love, show affection, talk about matters of the heart, and was verbally and physically abusive.

Growing up my dad never told me he loved me. He never told me he was proud of me. He never showed me affection. I can't tell you how

39

many times I was told, "You're a loser just like your mother," "You're lazy," "You're weak," "You're clueless," and called me other expletives. My dad would think it was funny to surprise me and randomly punch me in my arms. I would be walking into the kitchen and "Thud." Sometimes it was so hard I would cry. Perhaps, the bruises on my arms were meant to be continual reminders of who had the utmost power and control.

For years and years, I was berated. I was made to feel worthless, less than, and a nobody. I could do nothing right in his eyes. I had the self-esteem the size of a pinhead. I was infested with toxic shame. I hurt so deeply that as I became older, I cut myself on my arms, naively thinking that the seething pain could mysteriously escape. The pain never escaped. I had to grin and bear it. Not only was home difficult but my peers were ruthless.

I was twelve. It was the night before the first day of school. I was excited and nervous at the same time. I folded my clothes nice and neat for the adventure that lie ahead for the next day. I hoped it would be a good year. I hoped for a great teacher. I wished for new friends. I was ready to go for it.

My brothers and I were waiting at the bus stop. We were the last one. I could see the bus coming from a distance. My heart began to pound. The bus driver opened the doors and my smile instantly turned to a frown. The whole bus was chanting, "Nerds, nerds, nerds!" I wanted to run away as fast and far as I could but I couldn't. With my head held low, I mustered enough strength to find the first empty seat. There was no place that was safe. Not even school.

I was considered socially lame and bullied all the way up to highschool. I was made fun of because of my "coke-bottled" glasses. I was made fun of because of my "chicken legs" and my funny braces. I was made fun of because I wore dirty clothes to school. There were times when bullies knocked me down in the school hallways, with my books scattering everywhere. Thank goodness for a couple of misfit friends that made life tolerable. But there were some kids who were relentless.

Music, AIDS, and Jesus

Around the age of fifteen, I started listening to hard, heavy, anger-filled, and mosh-pit-inducing music, like Black Sabbath, Metallica, Pantera, Megadeth, Testament, and others. I think in some strange ways, they saved my life. They could relate to my anger, disillusionment, pain, hurt, and bitterness. I felt listened to and validated. They became my friends. Around this time is also when I received my first electric guitar. Playing music became an outlet for me and gave me a sense of purpose. It helped distract me temporarily from my pain and emptiness.

I learned to play guitar very quickly. In just a few years, I was in a band opening up for national acts. Although I had an amazing band, a model for girlfriend and a few people who cared about me, I was still depressed all the time. Of course, no one knew it. Perhaps they did but depression, emotional pain, and past wounding is not something anyone talked about. We live in much more therapeutic culture where it is more common. Back then, I remember longing for just one person to ask, "Mark, are you doing okay?" No one did. Eventually, all of the chaos, confusion, and pain became too much. I wanted to end my life. I was sick of it. I was empty, depressed and did not see the point to life.

About this time my twin brother became a Christian. He was quite zealous of his newfound faith. He constantly told me about Jesus and how much God loved me. But, I did not care. "Jesus, who the heck is Jesus?" I thought. I wanted to do my own thing. I thought that religious stuff was weird. But something was stirring in my heart. Or, I should say *someone* was stirring my heart. That someone was Jesus.

So as to avoid appearing uncool, I read some of the Bible when no one was looking. I wanted to know who this mysterious Jesus character was. Could he really be the answer to what my heart was desperately searching for? Could Jesus heal my pain and set me free, like my brother said? While I was contemplating Jesus, the Bible, and the Christian religion, I was having these vivid dreams of God calling me but all I did was run from Him. Aslan was apparently on the move and he wanted my heart. He wanted my life.

It seemed the more I got closer to the things of God, the crazier and more chaotic my internal and external world became. My mind felt like it was going crazy. Then, as a way to solve the dilemma of impending madness, I tried killing myself in one of the most twisted ways possible; I tried to get AIDS. I will spare you the X-rated details. Unfortunately, my mind and soul was desperately sick and I wished to no longer live. I engaged in risky behavior and hoped I would die a slow death.

Finally, there was a breaking point. One night, as I about to go to bed, I saw three red manifestations. At the time, I assumed they were evil spirits. I couldn't move. I tried to call out to my brother who was in the next room but I couldn't speak. I was terrified. I then closed my eyes and I did the only spiritual thing I knew how to do, which was to call out to Jesus, "Jesus, save me." I opened my eyes and guess what? They were still there. I know, it would have been nice if my spiritual trick worked. But, it didn't. I just lied there in my bed. Hoping, wishing, and praying for a miracle.

The next thing I knew I woke up in the morning. As soon as I got up, I was in panic. My heart was racing. I was sweating profusely. I was sobbing uncontrollably. I ran to my brother's room. I told him my story. He instantly said to me, "Mark, we wrestle not against flesh and blood, but against principalities, against powers, against the rulers of the darkness of this world, against spiritual wickedness in high places". I later realized he was quoting Ephesians 6:12 (KJV). He then talked to me once again about how Jesus wanted to save and deliver me. But, I was not yet ready.

I know what you are thinking, I must have been on drugs. Nope. I didn't do drugs. I don't you blame for being suspicious. Looking back on it, I am skeptical of my own experience. Could it really have been demons? It is interesting to note that researchers may call what I experienced *sleep paralysis*. It is an experience that can happen when a person is awake or about to go to sleep. They can see or hear things that may not be there but can result in a fear response. Researchers consider it a natural phenomenon, although they are not exactly sure why it happens. Religious people consider it a demonic event. Whatever it was, it left an indelible mark in my life; a mark that I could not ignore.

Tragedy, Trauma, and Triumph

A week later, I reached my breaking point (yes, I was stubborn). I was in a field not too far from our house, reflecting on my life and the events that kept happening to me. Then, I realized I had enough. I lifted my hands in the air and I spoke my last words of surrender. With tears in my eyes I said, "God, I am sick and tired of being sick and tired. If you are real, show yourself to me." It was at that moment, the uncontrolling love of God filled me wish his holy and healing presence. I was saturated with a love I never known before. It was tangible. It was thick. It covered me like a blanket on cold, breezy day. My old life was gone. I was a new creation. I was a phoenix who rose from the ashes.

Not to long after I was baptized in a lake and came up out the water praising and worshipping God. I remember fasting that day because I wanted all that God had for me. There was no looking back. It was awesome. I had a new life. I was overwhelmed with the love of God. His closeness was too much for me to handle sometimes. I would break down sobbing feeling a love that I had never felt before. Unfortunately the fairy tale ended pretty quickly.

Saved into a Cult

I was saved in a Oneness Pentecostal Church. That was the church my twin brother was going to. For many of you who don't know, that group could be found in the cult section of your local Christian bookstore (although some Christians are warming up to them as fellow believers). I was immediately thrown into a communal world where women were not supposed to wear pants. Women were not allowed to trim or cut their hair. Men were not allowed to have long hair or even facial hair. A person was not truly saved unless they were baptized by immersion, in the name of Jesus only and not the Father, Son and Holy Spirit (hence, the name by outsiders as *Jesus Only Folk*). They must be filled with the Holy Spirit as evidenced by speaking in tongues (you weren't saved unless you did). I was also told not to fellowship with Trinitarians because Oneness Pentecostals do not believe in the Trinity. I was in this madness for about four years.

I thought I was saved. I met all the requirements of the church. But I had this nagging sense that I was still may spend eternity in hell. I later realized that the teaching of the church did not help with my cognitive dissonance. The pastor's weekly yelling, guilting, and shaming fit would always cause me to doubt my salvation. Every Sunday, he would say in angst, "I am preaching hard like this because I want you to be saved". Was I not saved to begin with? It was very confusing. I remember telling a preacher from the same denomination that I drank wine at a wedding. He told me I was in danger of hell fire. When would I work hard enough to be saved? I had gotten to the point where I thought I could not drink soda. Why? Because I thought I would defile the temple of the Holy Spirit. Can you imagine the bondage and fear I was in to think such thoughts? I got saved from one hell into another.

Something didn't feel right. All of the toxicity from the church started to get to me. Over time, I knew I wanted to get out. It was at this time someone told me about a Christian college called, Nyack College. I wanted to go so bad. I always wanted to learn and go to school but the pastor didn't want me to. He told me there was too much work to do at the church. He offered the possibility of distance learning through videos from his denomination. My heart was crushed. I felt trapped.

One day, after standing in the middle of an argument between the pastor and his wife, something snapped within me. I mustered up enough courage and told them I was leaving. I left for Nyack College about a month later.

Goodbye Brother

In our early years, my younger brother was one of the most loving, outgoing, creative, and intelligent people I had known. He was the life of the party, "the Man," as they say. He had tons of friends. Girls loved him. He was an amazing brother, friend, and fellow adventurer. That is, until the age of twenty-one, when something tragic happened that forever changed the course of his life and our lives as his family. I came home one day to find all my brother's belongings set outside at the curb. Of course, I found that very strange, so I went inside to ask him about this. What I found was my brother curled up in a ball, mumbling and incoherent. He had thrown out all of his belongings, but he had no idea why.

We soon learned that my brother was suffering a psychotic episode, the first of many. After that terrible day, he was never the same. My siblings and I were grief stricken, having lost forever the loving, creative, intelligent brother we had known. Over the following days, my brother insisted that people were trying to kill him. At one point, he even declared himself to be Jesus Christ. In a grotesque parody of Christ's baptism, my brother baptized himself in a dirty, bug-infested lake not too far from our home. He believed this cleansed him from sin and he announced himself as the "savior of the world." It was so hard to watch knowing that he was the one who needed saving.

Eventually, the doctors diagnosed my brother with one of the cruelest forms of mental illness: paranoid schizophrenia. Along with his diagnosis came an endless cycle of psychotic episodes followed by hospitalizations and stabilizing medications. At the time, I could not understand how a loving God could allow that to happen to him. Even after all my prayers, fasting, and begging God to heal my brother, he remained sick.

Just a few years ago, he stopped taking his medication, and his subsequent unstable behavior resulted in his incarceration. In prison, during a time when he was off his medication again, he murdered a fellow prisoner. He will never again set foot outside of prison walls.

RIP Mama

My mom was a smart, compassionate woman of strength. She did her best to raise us. Unfortunately, she was addicted to drugs as far back as I can remember. As you might imagine, that made it kind of hard to consistently love, protect, and take care of us. It is difficult to be emotionally attuned to your children when you are frantically trying to find out when and from where your next high is going to come. But she was my mom, the only one I had. I loved her and longed for her to be whole and well.

I became a Christian in my twenties. That is when I began praying fervently for my mother. Day after day, year after year, my heartfelt prayer was for God to save her and rid her of her debilitating addiction. Not only did I pray, but members of my church and other Christian friends also lifted her up in prayer on a regular basis. There were glimmering moments when I thought my mother had seen the light and had quit drugs, but those were fleeting. As the days and weeks went by, I grew tired of praying for her, but I never gave up. Then one day, the worst imaginable thing happened—she overdosed and died. I was devastated and heartbroken.

Life-Lessons Learned from out of the Ashes of Trauma
1. God is not the Mastermind of Evil

When people think about the concept of evil, they typically think of heinous and morally reprehensible acts like murder, rape, and genocide. While all of these acts are evil, the biblical concept of evil is much broader. Simply put, evil is anything contrary to the will of God and contrary to shalom, such as thoughts (Gen. 6:5), deeds (Prov. 5:22), desires (Rom. 6:12), spirits (Mark 3:11), etc. Suffering is an inner cognitive/emotional experience in reaction to such things. But suffering can also come about from non-evil events. For example, a child who is told to go to bed early by his parents may experience suffering, but the event of going to bed early is not necessarily an evil act. Where there is evil, suffering is usually not far behind; however, where there is suffering, evil is not always present. Let's glean some insights into the origin of evil and subsequent suffering from the parable of the wheat and the tares.

The Parable of the Wheat and the Tares

The gospel of Matthew was written to a community experiencing trauma. The people were dealing with identity concerns, religious pluralism, infighting, the government's abuse of power, social and economic injustice, and many other difficult issues. Like us, the community wrestled with how a great God could allow good and evil to exist simultaneously in and around the lives of believers. In Matthew, Jesus addresses the community's inner ache, curiosity, and questions:

> *Jesus told them another parable: "The kingdom of heaven is like a man who sowed good seed in his field. But while everyone was sleeping, his enemy came and sowed weeds among the wheat, and went away. When the wheat sprouted and formed heads, then the weeds also appeared.*
>
> *The owner's servants came to him and said, "Sir, didn't you sow good seed in your field? Where then did the weeds come from?"*
>
> *"An enemy did this," he replied.*
>
> *The servants asked him, "Do you want us to go and pull them up?"*

> *"No," he answered, "because while you are pulling the weeds, you may uproot the wheat with them. Let both grow together until the harvest. At that time I will tell the harvesters: First collect the weeds and tie them in bundles to be burned; then gather the wheat and bring it into my barn." (Matt. 13:24–30)*

The Real Origin of Evil

Just as the servants in the parable were curious as to where the harmful weeds came from, we are curious as to where the evil and hardship in our lives come from. Because of the all the trauma that happened to me, I also needed to make sense of what happened. I needed to know if God was behind and planned my abusive childhood, my brother's illness, or mother's death. If God was and did, then it would be extremely hard to love him with all of my heart, mind and soul. The brain and spirit demand coherence. We turn again to the parable for some insights into possible origin of our suffering.

The Enemy

The owner of the field knew the origin of the evil weeds, for he said, in verse 28, "An enemy did this." The servant knew that the owner was not the originator, creator, or cause of the evil that happened to him, just as God is not the originator, creator, or cause of the evil that happens to us. Thomas Long writes, "It should first be heard as the powerful good news that it is. Evil is God's enemy. Not God's instrument, not God's counterpart, not something about which God is indifferent. Evil is God's enemy, period."[1]

God isn't joyfully working behind the scenes, orchestrating overdoses, murders, thefts, genocide, rape, and other horrific events. There are other dynamics at play when bad things happen to good people such as satanic or adversarial forces, and people's freewill choices.

In our modern era, Satan tends to be something relegated to horror movies and TV shows but the Bible is very clear: Satan, literally meaning *adversary* in Hebrew, does exist. According to 1 Peter 5:8, the enemy "prowls around like a roaring lion looking for someone to devour." Richard Beck, author of *Reviving Old Scratch: Demons and the Devil for Doubters and the Disenchanted*, defines Satan as "that which is adversarial to the kingdom of God."[2] He goes on to write that "while Christians might disagree about the exact nature of the forces arrayed against the kingdom, we recognize these forces as real and active in the world, forces that need to be fought and resisted."[3] Satan, in whatever force, form, person, structure, or guise he exists, should be taken seriously. Adversarial forces are witty, scheming, and plotting (2 Cor. 2:11), tempts people (Matt. 4:1; 1 Cor. 7:5), and tries to thwart the work of God in people's lives (1 Thess. 2:18).

---

[1] Thomas G. Long, What Shall We Say? Evil, Suffering, and the Crisis of Faith (Grand Rapids: Eerdmans, 2014), 133.
[2] Richard Allan Beck, Reviving Old Scratch: Demons and the Devil for Doubters and the Disenchanted (Minneapolis: Augsburg Fortress, 2016), 8.
[3] Ibid.

Tragedy, Trauma, and Triumph

Free Will

We can't blame everything on Satan ... or God. While satanic influence and other people's choices may be contributing factors, we also need to be courageous enough to ask ourselves how our own choices have led to our suffering. There are times when we are our own worst enemy. We are prone to planting weeds in the garden of our hearts and lives, sabotaging God's seeds of faith, hope, and love. In all my years of working with clients and congregants, I have found that asking ourselves how we might have contributed to our suffering is one of the most difficult questions to consider. It is much easier to point the finger at an ex, God, or Satan, and blame them for everything.

It could take many months' work before a client is ready for such a difficult, introspective journey. It certainly took me a while before I could ask myself the hard questions. Eventually, I found enough strength and courage and started praying one of the most "dangerous" prayers a Christian can pray. The prayer is found in Psalm 139:23–24: "Search me, God, and know my heart; test [examine] me and know my anxious [troubled] thoughts. See if there is any offensive [ôtseb in Hebrew, which can mean "mental or emotional suffering"] way in me, and lead me in the way everlasting." The more God revealed to me, the more God was able to heal.

The reality is that we have sin-filled crevices in our soul, and because of that, we don't always do the things we ought to, to ensure a successful relationship. Because we have pockets of selfishness, pride, lust, and greed, and, perhaps, deep wounds from past traumas, we unwittingly contribute to the breakup and our own heartbreak. If we know what the sin crevices are filled with, we can ask God to dig them out and fill them with his goodness, beauty, and truth. Asking the hard questions is not an exercise meant to condemn us or make us feel ashamed, but to help us be Christlike and succeed in relationships in the future.

God?

I tend to resonate with the owner in the parable. God is not the master designer of evil or devastating events. The servants knew the character of the owner because they asked, in Matthew 13:27, "Didn't you sow good seed in your field?" God, who is portrayed as the owner, is good (all the time) and he sows only good seed. Another metaphor, used in Luke 6:43, says, "No good tree bears bad fruit, nor does a bad tree bear good fruit." It is reasonable to assume that God, who is the all-good Tree of Life, would not produce bad fruit. And, finally, God offers us "living" (John 4:10) and fresh water. James 3:11 says, "Can both fresh water and salt water flow from the same spring?" God's water contains no impurities. He is good all the time, bears only good nutritious fruit, and is the purest and freshest water imaginable. God doesn't cause evil. God is love.

2. An Uncontrolling God Has Always Been with Me

Where was God when I was a scared little boy whose sense of security was smashed when his parents divorced? Where was God when my mother was doing drugs and my brothers and I were neglected?

Tragedy, Trauma, and Triumph

Where was God when fear and violence seemed to be the norm in our home? Where was God when kids bullied me in school? Where was God when my brother became mentally ill and eventually murdered someone? Where was God when I was poisoned by toxic religion? Where was God when my mother died from a drug overdose? God was with me.

One of the most liberating spiritual truths I have experienced in my walk with God is the truth that God didn't plan or cause the evil and suffering in my life. For the longest time, although a part of me knew God as loving, another part of me was angry at God. I could not understand how a loving God could meticulously plan such cruelty in my life. Thankfully, I have come to realize that due to God's loving nature, God does not dictate every action, reaction, or happening on this planet. Actually, it is not that God can do so but chooses not to, it is that God can't.

Because God's nature is love, there are some things that God cannot do. God does not override our free will, therefore he cannot single-handedly control people. Since God is love, love must preserve the sanctity of free will even at the cost of what that will may freely choose. To disregard and usurp free will is to cease being loving. God did not will the suffering in my life and therefore, God is not responsible. I can feel confident and assured that God is doing everything he can to maximize the good and minimize evil in not just my life, but every creature God has created.

Where was God when I was scared, confused, and abused little boy? God was seeking to comfort me and speak life and hope in my heart for better days. God was grieved at the choices my parents were making and out of his love for them was continually convicting and wooing them towards wholeness. Where was God when my mother was taking the last pill to end her life? God was grieving and non-coercively attempting to steer her towards wiser and more loving options. Where was God when my brother murdered his cellmate? God was angry at the injustice of the demonic prison system. God was grieved that one of his children was dead. God was saddened that my brother became less human that day. God has also not given up and continually seeks to restore my brother to a right mind and a healed heart. God is also with me; empowering me to hope and refract God's love with whom I am with, and wherever I may go.

3. We Need Connection with Others

While singing a worship song that was all about needing God, and God alone, I found myself needing to stop mid-chorus. Surprised at what was happening, I began to tear up. I realized I could no longer sing the lyrics with authenticity. I began to feel overwhelmed with heavy guilt and shame. I bowed my head and uttered something to myself I never expected to say: "God is not all I need."

Even though I was praying, fasting, reading the Bible, and submitting myself to God, I still hungered for something more—a real-life, flesh-and-blood human being or two who could compassionately enter my incessant loneliness and pain with me. I needed wit(h)nesses, people who made time to be compassionately present and wholeheartedly with me; not afraid to enter my dark experiences; and witness my sorrow and pain.

Of course, we need God, but God is not all we need. We have God-designed aches and hungers that God alone cannot fill, one of which is human connection. Even monks, priests, and nuns do life together; they are not off in a cave somewhere like a bunch of self-sufficient hermits.

Relationships are the entire thrust of the Christian faith. The Old and New Testaments are crammed with evidence that relationships are the very reason for our existence. God, who is a relational Trinity, exists in a threefold state of connection, equality, and love, and he wanted to extend that blessedness to humans. Not only that, God experiences profound parental pleasure when seeing us relate intimately and lovingly with each other. God loves it when we are like him.

While, ironically, our deepest pain comes from wounds inflicted by other people, other people also provide the most healing and growth. While God heals us directly through his Spirit (the vertical pathway), he also heals us indirectly through the wit(h)ness of other people (the first horizontal pathway). James 5:16 (AMP) says, "Therefore, confess your sins to one another [your false steps, your offenses], and pray for one another, that you may be healed and restored. The heartfelt and persistent prayer of a righteous man (believer) can accomplish much [when put into action and made effective by God—it is dynamic and can have tremendous power]."

Finding healing in community is not an alternative or fallback plan for those who do not have enough faith in God. It is a biblical imperative and part of God's gold standard for successful healing and living life to its fullest. Finding people to share your story with and experiencing their authentic, loving wit(h)ness as a result will allow you to grieve whatever losses you have experienced in life. Prioritizing the vertical relationship with God is vital, but you will also need to find a caring and praying community in which you can be gut-wrenchingly open and honest.

4. Shame Can Be Toxic

One of the emotions that zapped the zest out of my life was shame. Guilt is an emotion experienced after one has done something wrong, whereas shame is an experience that communicates to an individual that he or she is something wrong. Shame can send the message to us that we are unlovable, tainted, dirty, flawed, and no good. Shame causes us to weigh twenty-five, fifty, or seventy-five pounds more than we actually weigh in our spirits. Lewis Smedes writes that shame is "a vague, undefined heaviness that presses on our spirit, dampens our gratitude for the goodness of life, and slackens the free flow of joy. Shame ... seeps into and discolors all our other feelings, primarily about ourselves, but about almost everyone and everything else in our life as well."[4]

On many occasions shame is guilt gone rogue and has nothing to do with the oxygen of heaven. When referring to the inner emotional experience we have when we miss the mark (sin) regarding our actions, nonactions, and thoughts, I prefer the term healthy guilt or the biblical

---

[4] Lewis B. Smedes, Shame and Grace: Healing the Shame We Don't Deserve (San Francisco: HarperSanFrancisco, 1993), 1.

phrase godly sorrow. Worldly sorrow (unhealthy shame) leads to death, but godly sorrow leads to life with no yucky residue (2 Cor. 7:10). Godly sorrow is an inner remorse one feels because of sinful behavior or inaction and has a built-in plea for action, which prioritizes relationships and moves a person to right their wrongs.

I internalized the disgust that my father and my peers had toward me and projected it toward myself. If everyone else didn't like me, then why would I like myself. Actually, I hated myself. The poison of shame was the very reason I tried to kill myself. It was part of the reason why I would cut myself. Shame kept me alone and isolated. It was deadly.

Toxic shame is a debilitating emotion that has no rightful place in the heart of a child of God. Shame is one of the most harmful emotions that exist within the human experience, especially when it festers and darkens one's view of oneself, God, and others. It contributes to much of our suffering and catapults us into addictions, self-harm, and harming others. I know those are bold statements, but there is plenty of research to back them up.

When thinking about unhealthy shame, I am reminded of clogged up fuel injectors. In cars, fuel injectors are tiny valves that open and close in response to electrical signals from the car's computer. They open, and release fuel to the engine. Sometimes, though, grime and dirt build up in the valves, which causes the car not to accelerate or even start. Shame, condemnation, and harshness toward yourself can clog your spiritual and emotional arteries. They can block the divine fuel of freedom and joy from running smoothly through your heart, keeping you bound and joyless, unable to grieve well. They have no place in your life and are contrary to Jesus's redemptive work on your behalf. You have permission to love yourself boldly, deeply, and compassionately.

6. It is Okay to Love Ourselves

You need to love yourself. Does that sound weird? Does that sound heretical? Like New Age sewage? Are we allowed to love ourselves, as Christians? Isn't it sinful or selfish? Don't we love ourselves too much already, especially if we live in the spoiled, hyper-pleasure-focused Western society?

First, it is not sinful and selfish to love ourselves. It is sinful and selfish if we elevate our love for ourselves over and above God and others, which is another word for pride and narcissism. Second, I don't think we love ourselves as much as we think we do. America's daily consumption of drugs and alcohol and dreadful diet of processed sugars while obsessively binge-watching oxymoronic fake/reality TV shows is not loving ourselves. Engaging in such activities can actually be harmful, and in some instances hateful toward ourselves.

Unfortunately, in my work as a pastor and a therapist, I find Christians to be some of the most self-deprecating people I have ever met. I was one of them. Not only do many of us not love ourselves, we do not even like ourselves. This is probably because of a lack of solid teaching on the subject or an overemphasis on "the depravity of man" types of doctrines. When was the last time you heard a sermon called "The Three Biblical Steps to Loving Yourself"? My guess is you have never heard anything even remotely close. This lack of self-love saddens me tremendously, and I am sure it grieves the heart of God that we ignore the second part of the greatest commandment in Mark 12:31, to "love your neighbor as yourself." And that is to our detriment. If anyone should be connoisseurs of a holistic love, it should be Christians whose God is love.

I have learned to love myself as God loves me. Trust me, it is a whole lot better to love ourselves than to beat ourselves up and be infested with shame. Imitate the relational style of the Father of love, exterminate the relational style of the father of lies. You're either treating yourself with compassion or condemnation, with relenting hope or a negative nope, with tender forgiveness or toxic bitterness. Love yourself as God loves you.

7. We Need to Forgive to Live

Forgiveness is not forgetting, pretending, or a fancy word for psychological suppression. Forgiveness is a prayerful process of surrendering to God's will and making a choice to release the debt we feel the injurer owes us because of how deeply he or she hurt us. True forgiveness does not deny but accepts the full impact of the injuring partner's choices and makes a decision to let go and let God perform his transformational work in our lives. Forgiveness is also a powerful gift from God that releases us from the poison of the bitterness of unforgiveness.

Although it has taken years, I have finally forgiven my parents, my step-father, life, God, myself, and anyone else who has ever hurt me. I realized if God has forgiven all of my sins and continues to do so, then how could I withhold forgiveness for anyone else? Even after all of my wanderings and continual shutting my ears to God's loving voice, God always gives me another chance. Moment-to-moment God offers me his forgiveness and healing graces. While I may not have reconciled with all those who have caused me pain and became close companions, I have made a choice to forgive them and set myself free.

God did not command us to forgive to make life hard but to emancipate us from a hard life and propel us toward a future where love is easily expressed and felt. The apostle Paul lovingly encourages us to "make every effort to live in peace with everyone" (Heb. 12:14) and cautions us "that no bitter root grows up to cause trouble and defile many" (v. 15). If we choose to harbor the bitter root and negative energy of unforgiveness, then we are wasting additional energy to keep those destructive elements at bay so they don't spill out and harm ourselves and other people. But what if you forgave, released yourself from the negative energy, and instead used the freed-up emotional energy in positive ways? That energy could be used to love yourself, God, and others with much greater capacity. There is no greater joy than to love and be loved freely!

Conclusion

Thank you for taking a journey with me, entering into my trauma, my losses and some of the life-changing truths that has transformed my life. Life is not easy. Life is also not fair. But, we can take confidence that God's uncontrolling love is trustworthy; it never fails and always seeks to bring us and the world toward greater experiences of shalom.

Mark Karris is an ordained pastor, licensed marriage and family therapist, musician and all around biophilic. He is the author of
Divine Echoes: Reconciling Prayer with the Uncontrolling Love of God (Quoir, 2018) and Season of Heartbreak: Healing for the Heart, Brain, and Soul (Kregel, 2017).
MarkGregoryKarris.com

The Ever-Present God of Uncontrolling Love
Janyne McConnaughey, PhD

The people of the church smiled when the small bundle of energy with blond hair flew by on her way to claim her piece of Sunday candy from the kind usher who always waited for her at the back of the sanctuary. When she was very small, he made her stay with him until the candy was gone so she wouldn't choke, but as she got older, there really was no stopping her. She was off to find her friends whom she had known since she was in the nursery. The church was their home. They had watched it being built from the ground up and claimed the basement as their own.

It was good that Jeannie had so many who thought they were part of her family. Her father adored her but was very busy as pastor of a growing church. Her mother never understood how to or at least wasn't able to be the mother this child needed. She often handed the responsibility of little Jeannie off to her eldest brother. He still watches over her, 65 years later.

It took a village to raise this small child. Most were never aware of the tragedy that struck the family when she was sexually abused in a home daycare at the age of three. The doctor told her father that she would forget. No one ever talked about what happened. Her subconscious helped her repress the painful memory, but it lived on in her body and set her on a course that put her in danger again and again. Perpetrators seemed to sense that she was vulnerable and would never talk about what they did.

This was my story. It was the truth that my subconscious repressed until it exploded out of me at the age of 62. Fortunately I had listened to God's prompting and gone to therapy where I finally received the help I needed to process the extensive pain I held in my mind and body.

It was a three-year journey of healing—one that will probably continue for the rest of my life. I am thankful for the skillful care of a therapist who never doubted that I could heal and her determination to get me to a place where I could care for myself. God's direction in my healing process was clear, but she knew better than to even mention God for many, many months. It was complicated.

My relationship with the church and God were similar to a traumatized child whose caretakers were also the abusers. I relied on the church and God to care for me but at the same time was constantly tripping over the landmines of legalism, judgment, and perpetrators clothed in sheepskins. I depended on the church to care for me while fearing the betrayals that inevitably came. It was complicated.

The interesting part of the story was that I never doubted God loved me. I doubted that God provided protection for me but never doubted the love. My struggle centered around the idea of God as controlling—having a plan for my life which included the abuse was explored in my essay for the book, *Uncontrolling Love*.[1] My theology had trapped me into believing that I didn't have choices. I couldn't even die when I wanted to. Reading the original book, *The Uncontrolling Love of God*, was life changing and came at the point in my therapy when I needed to understand that God was weeping over me during every assault.[2] My perpetrators had free choice and chose evil, but it didn't mean that God wasn't doing everything possible to care for me. It took me some time to accept and grasp this truth. I had to come to terms with the fact that my care had been totally dependent on the ability and willingness of people to listen to the voice of God on my behalf. On this side of healing, I am thankful for those who did listen and step in to care for me in ways that probably saved my life. This is that story.

I can't even count the times my therapist and I stopped to reflect on how truly miraculous it was that I lived the life I lived. I annihilated every statistic for insecure attachment and childhood abuse. I was the

---

[1] See Chris Baker, et.al. *Uncontrolling Love*. (SacraSage Press: Nampa, ID, 2017).
[2] Thomas Jay Oord, *The Uncontrolling Love of God: An Open and Relational Account of Providence* (Downers Grove: InterVarsity Press, 2016),

poster child for resiliency, but it didn't mean that I wasn't suffering internally. Somehow, I had been married for 36 years (39 now), raised two competent adult children, and completed a 40-year career in education. As memory of abuse after abuse after abuse surfaced—from the age of three to twenty-three—the possibility of living the life I lived diminished. Yet it was true. We often discussed why that happened.

First, my family life was not chaotic like the homes of so many children who experience abuse. My mother did care for my physical needs. My father was the one who nurtured me. My brother was always there for me—though sometimes irritated by his pesky little sister. My home life lacked the emotional support of a mother, but it was not chaotic. My father was my hero until he died at the age of 100 near the end of my therapy journey, but we never talked about what happened and he never knew it continued.

Second, I was just about the most tenacious and creative child on the planet. Unable to bear the pain, and without emotional support from my mother, my subconscious began to split parts of me off in order to live. By the time I entered therapy, I had a complete dissociative system with over twenty alters (mostly children who were frozen in my psyche by the trauma). I believe because of the lack of chaos in my family, I created a very functional system and while every personality was distinct and had a particular role, they all resembled the person everyone knew as Jeannie and then Janyne. Dissociation saved my life while putting me in danger. I could never have lived without splitting off the pain. I used the coping mechanism of dissociation to survive. To the world it looked like thriving, but it wasn't.

Both of these ways I survived were part of my family and internal system. They were never going to be enough. When I entered school, I had many teachers I confused by not 'working up to my potential,' but they cared about me in significant ways. I grew up in a family of educators and chose education for a career. It was probably more about the teachers who cared than anything else. Teachers are high on my list of ways I survived. Many of them were people of faith. I truly believe they saw me through the eyes of Jesus. I was possibly one of the neediest students in the room.

Last but not least, was the church—which at this point, I will discuss as an entity in and of itself—not as the body of Christ. From my earliest years, I understood the church put bread on our table. The church could vote and send us out into the wilderness without sustenance. We needed to be who the church expected us to be. The church could be capricious and turn against our family. As a child, I was unable to distinguish between the church as a whole and the people as individuals. It was confusing to have to fear the people who seemed to care about me, but that kind of fit my experiences as a whole. Church, God, and the people became one indistinguishable unit. One I feared and depended on all at the same time.

Like a child depends on family, I depended on the church. Even when I got old enough to leave, I made career choices that would continue my dependence on the church by teaching at Bible colleges. I gave up much of my personal identity to be who the church wanted me to be. I was diminished as a woman leader and accepted fundamentalist male domination for half of my career. Finally, after twenty years, I was betrayed and abandoned and I returned to the church of my heritage. It was better. I finished well, but retiring was fraught with anxiety over leaving the security of the church that had both abused and cared for me.

Now, two years later, I am to the point of unwinding 'the church' as an institution from 'the church' as the body of believers who truly did care for me. The people who cared are the final reason why I did not reap the full effects of my abuse. Those who failed are tragic counter-examples of who God desires us to be for each other, but the impact of those who didn't fail supersedes them.

I believe children who survive abuse within church contexts (or by people who profess faith) have a very difficult path ahead of them. The internalized shame is overwhelming. How is it possible for someone who sings the hymns with meaning on Sunday to abuse a child on Monday? Everyone holds them in esteem and the child is left with only one conclusion: What happened is my fault. To overcome this requires a huge number of counterexamples. That is what God provided to me in the people of the church—the ones who listened to God and got it right.

The kind usher with the candy is my symbol for counterexamples. His name was Mr. Counts, and my trust for him overcame my fear. He was probably not the first person to care for me in that church where I arrived as a newborn baby, but he is the one who is embedded in my emotional memories of childhood. He was always the example I clung to when others failed me. I will always believe God was trying to show me love through the pieces of candy in the pockets of this kind man. He was not the last to care about me.

There were two women who occasionally cared for me as a child. I have a picture of myself as a baby, sitting on the floor between them. We were all smiling. When I was fifty and the church was fifty, I went to an anniversary celebration and stayed with Freda. She had remained our family friend and kept track of my brothers and me. She was one of the few people who called my mother her friend, but she said, "If it hadn't been for your dad, you wouldn't have gotten any nurturing. Your mother should not have had children, but if she hadn't we wouldn't have you and your brothers."

She told me this long before I went to therapy, but I will always believe God led her to say this so I would know my relationship with my mother wasn't my fault. I needed to know that when my story began to explode from me. My unmet attachment needs would have caused me to need and seek attention. My perpetrators knew it, but it was never my fault. God spoke through this longtime friend to help me understand.

When I was in early elementary school, my family had a cabin on the Church of the Nazarene campgrounds in New Mexico. This expanded my world of those who cared for me and provided a safe place to explore. My father would often go there to work and I was his constant companion. Everyone knew me and I knew everyone. I always saw delight in the eyes of the people who watched over me. When my bother broke his arm and they couldn't find me to take me to town with them; in the confusion of some thinking others had me, I was left by myself. I had some scary moments, but I knew if I could get to the snack shop I would find people who would take care of me. I was right. They circled me in dismay and bought me a treat. They were the arms of God that wrapped a frightened little girl in a circle of care.

It was at that same campground that I thought I understood my dark cloud to be the same as the burden that Christian carried in *Pilgrim's Progress*. There is much to this part of my story, but suffice it to say, my quest to solve the problem of the dark cloud took me to the altar during camp meeting. It was there I met a woman who I realize now looked remarkably like my therapist some fifty plus years later. While at the altar, she took my hands in hers and prayed for me. I thought she was an angel. In many ways she was. No other adult seemed to notice the small eight-year-old child who came to the altar—not even my parents. I still had the dark cloud hovering over me when I left the altar, but I had felt the touch of God in the touch of the angel who cared for me. I was small, but she noticed me. Many years later, I would instantly trust my therapist because a small child inside of me thought she had found her angel again.

As I grew older, I started going to church camp. I went every year from the time I was ten until I went to college. The last few years, I spent multiple weeks by attending my own camp and then serving as a counselor in two other camps. I really cannot overemphasize the importance of camp in my life. In addition, I would spend a week at camp meeting. There was one common denominator in all of these weeks—my counselors.

There were many counselors who cared for me over those years but none as important as the three women I called the Marhad sisters. I rotated between the three sisters and they all invested in my life. Part of me knew no fear and was bound and determined to push every boundary and rule. I wasn't a bad kid; I just needed attention and ditching chapel and sneaking out of the cabin at night filled that need—besides the fact that my friends and I had great adventures together. These three women always shook their heads but smiled.

I always lived in two parts—the one who lived and the one who held the pain. I am sure every counselor wondered how such a fun-loving teenager could suddenly fall into a seemingly bottomless pit of despair. I didn't understand it either, but I desperately needed my counselors to care about me.

These three women didn't walk away at the end of the week. They kept in touch and when we were in the town where they lived, they often invited me to go to lunch or come to their house. They were my lifelines during those years when I appeared to be a very healthy teenager, but my subconscious believed I was demon possessed because of all the voices in my head.

I never fell into the common behaviors that often trap those who have been abused as children. Although I went into marriage believing I had been complicit, I had not. Nothing that happened to me at the hands of the perpetrators was my choice. I was not sexually promiscuous. I had one high school boyfriend and it was a healthy relationship—until my anger issues surfaced. I also did not fall into the trap of soothing the turmoil inside of me with drugs or alcohol. I understood my brain was how I was surviving. I was not going to do anything to harm my best asset. That did not change the fact that I was dealing with turmoil that I couldn't name or understand.

Without those who invested in my life, the result could have been very tragic. In my young adult years, that was exactly what happened and I eventually drove to a cliff and tried to end my life. It was on that cliff that a man saw my car skid off the road and then watched as I ran and stood at the edge. I have no doubt that he was on that road that day because God needed him to be there. I was beyond listening to the voice of the God whom I did not believe protected me. I needed a human being to convince me to step back from the edge. At first I screamed in fear that he was there to rape me, but he knew exactly what to say and do to help me understand the danger in which I had placed myself. I did turn, but slipped off the edge, grabbed and held tree roots, and was then pulled to safety.

There is so much that happened inside my soul that day, but the importance of the event for this part of my story is that, once again, God could not stop what happened because it was a choice of freewill that was used for evil. It was the awful betrayal that sent me to the cliff, but God wept with me and then chased me up the mountain and called in support to convince me not to end my life.

It took two years of therapy and gaining an understanding in the uncontrolling God of love to bring me to the place where I can look over the landscape of my life and understand that God was with me every single moment. I was both strong and fragile. God knew I needed people who would both believe in me and protect me. The many who cared about me are too numerous to mention, but it is important to understand how dependent I was on the care others gave me and how important it was that they were the arms of God that reached out to me in human form.

When I came down from that mountain, I had built an entire new layer to protect myself from those who preyed upon me while presenting godly faces to the world. I was in survival mode and the only place I knew how to survive was the church and church-related schools and ministries. I had learned how to keep myself safe there and that is exactly what I did for the remainder of my working life. I trusted few but lived as though I did. No one ever knew unless I leaked.

Leaking was a problem. I had methods to keep the pain from seeping out around the edges, but sometimes those methods failed and I needed help. In thirty-five years there were only three who knew some of the pain I had experienced—the pain that I believed was my own fault. I controlled myself with that belief.

In every place I lived or worked there were always some who appreciated my leadership skills but also understood that I had tendencies to go rogue—either in impulsive decisions or out of despair and frustration. They often stepped in to provide a buffer of protection. They didn't always understand me, but they knew my heart and cared deeply. I would not have survived without them.

Those who truly knew me saw my vulnerable and fragile side. One of my closest friends once said, "Janyne, you are always laughing, but no one really knows."

No, for the most part they didn't. Every structure I built was for the purpose of hiding. I was a pro at hiding. If I ever trusted someone enough to share any of the story I actually kept in conscious memory, it was a very big deal. Despite my serious trust issues, God surrounded me with women whom I truly did trust. As I began to share my story with them during my healing journey, I am sure many things I did finally made sense.

I was a survivor. I fought my way through life while hiding a broken and hurting three-year-old in a cage inside my soul. Like many others, I was reeling from traumatic childhood experiences. I lived out those experiences through triggers, PTSD flashbacks, dissociation, anxiety, panic attacks, and debilitating depression. I listened to sermons that convinced me it was spiritual failure and worked even harder to control what I couldn't understand. All the while, I filled my world with laughter and professionalism, and I cared for others in all the ways I longed to be cared for. If I hadn't leaked occasionally and landed in bed with stress-related illnesses, I could have pulled it off perfectly.

In the midst, I was married. I married someone who I loved to the degree I could and believed would take care of me. I was absolutely correct. It is hard to imagine how hard we fought to survive the mental health tsunami that struck us in the 36th year of our marriage. With our children safely launched into adulthood, and my dad whom we cared for during the last five years of his life in a nursing home and, later, safely in heaven, our world quietly exploded. Without my husband's care, I would have needed to be institutionalized several times. We knew many marriages collapsed under similar strains, but our commitment to care for each other no matter what was strong.

I remember one day, just a year past college graduation, when I was job hunting and I heard God's voice tell me to go back to a place I had passed. I listened, and it was there that I met my husband. Most felt we were perfect for each other, while some warned him not to marry me. It seems that we were determined to prove those voices wrong. God knew we would need each other. I am glad we listened.

I can now clearly see that God was always there. I couldn't always believe that, but I now understand that God's love was present in every friend who cared about me. I have an unusually large number of these friends in my life. I always knew I was blessed to have so many who cared—what I didn't understand was how God was consistently showing his love for me through them.

Before I came apart, there was one important friend who walked into my life to prepare me for the journey of healing that was ahead of me. We both remember the day she came to my office and sat on my couch. During the first three years of our friendship, she helped me get into the physical shape that I would need in order to survive. She listened to me as my protective layers began to crack. She hugged me when I cried and played the piano to soothe the pain that neither of us fully understood. I slowly transformed into a part of me that had been tightly controlled for years, while the part who held the pain began to cry.

When my friend moved away, it was the moment of truth for me. I understood the dark cloud that had hovered over me my entire life had now descended in a way that I could no longer contain. I also understood my life had been overly dependent on those who cared for me, and it was time to understand why. I begged God to help me.

The day I walked into therapy, I was primed to do the work. God had used my friend to prepare me to accept the care I would receive. Without that transformational friendship, I would never have allowed myself to trust enough to heal.

God used the holding space of all my friends in order to help me survive. Now I had been placed in the care of a therapist who was going to acknowledge God's presence as she worked to help me heal. She wasn't just any therapist. She was the one God prompted me to call. It astounds me that she looks like the 'angel' who prayed for me as a child. She understood and trusted my sense of God prompting me in ways that brought the memories I needed to process to the surface. God, who had been watching over me since the day I was born, was going to bring the healing I cried for through the skill and care of a therapist.

My story is a tribute to how the body of Christ can stand in the gap for our hurting world. I do not say church here, because the care of one individual for another so often gets lost in church programs. While we can't individually help everyone, we can be open to God's prompting when a hurting soul walks into our lives. Maybe we don't even know they are hurting. Maybe we think we are simply enjoying a friendship while we toss them a lifeline. I doubt many understood the very important role they were playing in my life. I doubt we ever fully know the impact we are having when we decide to invest in each other.

As I began to unravel my story and understand God's working throughout my life, it became clear that God's power did not rest in control. God's power rested in the created humans who were willing to listen and act on his behest. No matter what God desires in our lives, the fulfillment is always going to depend on human choice—our own and those around us.

As terrible as the choices for evil were against me, the choices that brought protection and care into my life were far more powerful. They were the true display of God's uncontrolling love—given freely in response to the spirit of God in every believer. I could not have survived without the support of all who cared for me.

It is also true that God's love for me was displayed in the actions of those who made no profession of faith. I often felt safer in those circumstances where I didn't fear that harm would be done in religious guise. Even nature spoke to me as I healed. I also heard God's voice in popular songs and secular writings. God, it seemed, was not limited by man's preconceived religious boxes. I felt all of heaven and earth step up to help me heal.

My story is a modern-day miracle. I should not have been able to heal as I did in only three years. I understand the gift I have been given. I hear the pain of others in the private messages I receive thanking me for breaking the silence and giving them hope. My heart cries out against the stigma that causes them to delay seeking help.

I am thankful for the long line of those who cared for me—all those who are symbolized by the gentle and kind usher who had candy waiting for me in his pocket every Sunday. I would have loved him even without the candy because he smiled at me and complimented my new shiny shoes. I sensed I was safe, which surprises me. Maybe I saw Jesus looking at me through his eyes. We all need someone to look at us with Jesus' eyes. When we do this for others, we can change their lives forever.

Janyne McConnaughey, PhD, retired from a career in education that spanned forty years—from early-childhood educator to college professor—in order to heal from the effects of the childhood abuse she had suffered. During therapy, Janyne wrote her way to healing and now is redeeming her story by helping others to understand and heal from childhood trauma. Along with Brave: A Personal Story of Healing Childhood Trauma, Janyne is working on two forthcoming sequels. She also keeps busy blogging at Janyne.org, and guest blogging for other organizations that address childhood trauma. Janyne enjoys full-time RV living with her husband, Scott, at the edge of Garden of the Gods in Colorado Springs, Colorado, and treasures time she spends in the Seattle area with her children and grandchildren.

Deep Calls to Deep
Sharon R. Harvey

God's uncontrolling love is connected to our deepest places, our deepest desires, and our deepest moments. This is the story of my deepest depths: events of life which did not make sense, situations of loss, divorce, death, and disappointment. Surprisingly and refreshingly, God reached me by knowing the depths of my person—what it is that gives meaning and hope to me again and again—and by getting involved with me in the pursuit of those very personal joys. These words discuss the lonely struggle of coming to a new country, of pursuing ordination and being refused, of both accomplishment and rejection in academic work, of losing a marriage of 34 years, and of seeing my mother destroyed by a senseless car accident. It seeks to question how joy could come of all these events and indicates that having one who knows us intimately makes all the difference.

I sat cross-legged on the floor of the library reading the book in my hand. At age 15, I was now three years into experiencing culture shock as a result of moving to inner Kansas City from Haiti, where I had been born and spent my childhood. Thoroughly homesick, I longed for someone to understand my struggle. I felt like a fish out of water, as things were so different from the primitive country I had left. The sights, smells, and sounds of my upbringing had all but vanished. Modern society seemed to include very few deep relationships. I was scrambling to figure out how to be accepted by my peers but was also disillusioned with their values. There seemed to be no connection to the natural world—no sense of place or belonging, but rather a time consuming, relentless accumulation of things. People were in a hurry with few moments to cease activity or reflect.

At last I found it! A philosopher's words on the page in front of me spoke hope to my soul on the significance of place. Suddenly, I was transported beyond my present reality to Haiti again and comforted at the same time. Heidegger's words became my regular retreat from which to explore complexities of thought that none of my peers seemed to grasp. These were some of the deepest places of my life.

Somehow I survived the raging teenage hormones, a racially-charged school near the railroad tracks in Kansas City, and cultural adaptation. I never wanted to return to those years again. Hostility and profanity cloaked the hallways of my school. Our class would walk five blocks uphill to participate in outdoor sports; coming down, the gangs would kick rocks at the backs of my legs, cursing me on the way. They would say, "I'm gonna kill you," while the teacher rode past in her car, doing nothing.

Things were so bad that the principal would let me out of school ten minutes early so that I could get a head start running for home. I often came home crying and asking to go to another school because of the bullying that I experienced. I lived in fear and hated my life in the United States. If only I could go back to the country I loved. This situation was especially disconcerting and incomprehensible to me, as I had grown up color blind in Haiti. I could not understand how things could be so different in America, even after a civil rights victory. Once, while pulling my little sister in a wagon to a nearby dime store, I was threatened by some kids, and later a rock was thrown into my bedroom window. After that, I was afraid to go out in my community. Eventually, my parents moved to another neighborhood to get away from all the problems I was experiencing.

In my senior year, I had the opportunity to return to Haiti after six long years of being away. Every day I longed to go back home, and I saved my money to return. It was such a marvelous experience being there; but when I got on the plane to leave, I began to sob uncontrollably. I was bent over with tears falling onto my lap once the island slipped from view out of my window. I did not know when I would ever return to my country again. Suddenly my thoughts were interrupted by my peripheral vision indicating that someone across the aisle was leaning over trying to get my attention. I looked over, and in that moment realized for the first time that God existed and knew my name. Unbelievably, Stephanie, my very best friend from Haiti who had moved to Maryland and had lost complete contact with me, was on that same plane! How, in all the world, could she possibly be here on the same plane, in the same row, at the same time as I, singlehandedly outwitting the potentially uncontrollable agony of my soul? We nearly clobbered everyone's knees as we bolted for each other, landing in the aisle with a big hug. What a happy chatter we had in that hour ride to Miami. What a perfect gift from God! It was too good to be true! It still fills me with wonder when I recall that incredible, serendipitous, miraculous moment.

Furthermore, in my senior year, my faith was stabilized with Jesus, thanks to ordinary, ongoing ministries of a local Nazarene church, and I ended up going to a Nazarene college nearby. Someone along the way had said I couldn't be both a Christian and a philosopher, so I put Heidegger's thoughts far away on a back burner. I wasn't sure why that was supposed to be a problem, but I wanted to be God-honoring. Heidegger was totally out of my picture for over twenty years.

Those twenty years brought a lot of experiences to me. While in college I married a minister, completed my degree, and we ended up pastoring three churches in Missouri, Texas, and Oklahoma before going to Montréal, Québec to plant an English-speaking church. God graced us with two wonderful children—a son and daughter. Our family learned to boldly face the challenges of living in the North Country, choosing to love snow and to celebrate life in Canada. We had a little cottage just over the

Sharon R. Harvey

New York border on a Holiness Campground where we would go with our family to get away and make memories. The kids learned to ride their bikes under the tall trees along the river, and Camp Meeting played a vital role in our family's spiritual growth.

I led a lay training program for our multi-cultural Nazarene district, and my heart was becoming strangely warmed toward thoughts of being in the ministry as I saw a couple of our laymen going on to prepare for ordination. At an All-Canada Conference in Toronto, during a special song, I was overwhelmed by the Lord's presence and it was a precious experience. God was calling me. At the time, I had also been reading, "The Call," an essay that was later used for the Nazarene Handbook for ministerial candidates in Canada. Back in the car for the ride home, my Barbadian pastor and her husband had drifted off to sleep, and I was quietly asking God if this call on my life could be true. As I did, scenes flashed before me. I had always intended to go to seminary but had ended up in pastoral ministry with my spouse. I saw glimpses of God moving in my life all along the way toward this vocation. Eventually, my husband asked what I was thinking, and I was almost too scared to speak about it, but I ventured to express what was happening inside of me. Suddenly my pastor rose up in the back seat and stated that I was definitely "on" to start preaching every Sunday night!

Preaching began, and it was as if the messages flowed easily and naturally each week. I had a collection of sermons written in a notebook, and one snowy night I came out to my car and put my notebook on the top while I buckled my child in the back seat. I got in and had driven a few blocks when it dawned on me that I had forgotten my sermon book on top of the car. I pulled over instantly, but it was gone. I went back and forth several times looking for where the notebook may have fallen, but I didn't ever find it. It felt like I had lost something very special, and I was sad to not have the messages anymore. I could only hope that someone who needed the messages would find them. I realized then and there how much I was blessed to have a preaching ministry and how much those messages meant to me, personally.

It wasn't long after that when I achieved my local license and prepared to go to the ministerial board to further pursue ordination. This was a very special day when I articulated my call to a long table of men from several upper states and some from Canada. I was then asked to leave the room. After a bit of a wait, someone came and informed me that my ministerial license was declined. I was not called to a preaching ministry. Stunned, my mind was racing. What had happened? Was it because I was a woman, and did not articulate the call in terms that men could understand? I did not anticipate this rejection. Thinking back, I recalled one man in the room arguing in my defense saying, "She has fruit from her ministry, and the man we approved before her did not."

Most likely he was commenting on a Rwandan ministry I started in Montréal when, following the genocide, I amassed huge medicine donations from pharmaceutical companies and churches and shipped them to Rwanda. Out of that emerged local unity services in Montréal for Rwandan refugees. As a result, I started a French Bible Study through which a woman got saved, joined the church, and was serving on the board.

Thoroughly numbed from the news, I went home. For three days I was unable to do much, extremely distraught by the turn of events, and nothing could console me. It was like losing a treasure that I had valued, and I was stymied by the event. I never questioned my call, but what was I to do now that it seemed unanswerable? These were some of the deepest searching moments of my life.

Sitting out in the living room later in the week, my husband asked, "Why don't you consider going to graduate school?"

I responded, "Well, what would I study?"

He began to ask about things, one by one, "Business...? Science...? History...?"

Each category was met with an unexcited shrug.

"How about English...? Literature...? Philosophy...?"

A slight smile curled on my lips, and I had a faraway gaze as I was thinking.

"What is it?" he asked, excitedly.

"What?" I asked.

He continued: "You perked up! What were you thinking about just now?"

"Oh, it's just Heidegger," I said.

He exclaimed, "Heidegger! Who's that?"

I tossed my head with a laugh, "Oh just some dead philosopher that I used to love."

He nearly shouted, "That's it! Go study Heidegger!"

And that's what I did. I loved being a student. Those were clearly the most thought provoking days of my life, trudging through snow to the university, wondering if anything would ever become of my choice to study Heidegger. Ironically, I was finding how important philosophy's claims were for refining my faith and observed that it actually strengthened my resolve to serve the Lord. I was happy and fulfilled, finding places to speak and teach, doing research and writing, and eventually finishing my Master's degree.

Our job ended up taking us to Idaho after 15 years in Canada, and the family packed up and headed west. Having started a doctoral program in Montréal, I was disappointed to leave it, but thankfully the town where we were located had a university. Soon after moving there, I was able to continue my doctoral work. For the present, I was exploring open theism and the environment, looking for resources to construct a theological ethics of the environment. I first became aware of open theism from my father before it was ever popularized. A Nazarene minister, he used to mark the margins of his Bible with a big "C" whenever he found "contingency" with regard to God. He was a thinker, as was my mom, and I always enjoyed a good theological discussion with them. Then, while I was teaching a university class in Montréal, a student of mine from Ontario knew Clark Pinnock and wanted to write her paper on his version of open theism. Upon reading her paper and revisiting the topic with my dad, I began to look for any current Nazarene scholars exploring open theism, and Tom Oord was doing this, in Idaho. After moving to Idaho, I contacted Oord to see if anyone was linking open theology with the environment. He encouraged me to pursue it and supplied me with a great deal of literature to read. Learning about it made me realize how much we blame God when there are also human responsibility, the Devil, and natural causes to consider. I was attracted to a God who limited Himself, thinking that because of His example, we too should practice self-limitation with regard to the natural world.

Studying open theism was fascinating, albeit not always well received. Later on it seemed to be more of a threat to my portfolio with Christian people—a risk I had not expected. On one occasion, I was denied a job at a Christian university and was told that is was primarily because a majority of the committee reacted to my association with that topic. Regardless of those negative reactions, I found that open theism answered the hardest philosophical questions on the problem of suffering and evil. I felt that as a theology, a belief in open theism did not negatively affect the doctrine of salvation, which was definitely in its favor. Other prominent doctrines do affect the doctrine of salvation, which deter access to God. I also liked that some open theists acknowledged the role of Satan. Having grown up in Haiti with my parents' stories on Voodoo conversions, it was good to see that this theology had import for lesser developing nations as well as for demonic oppression that is becoming more noticeable here in the United States.

As I sought to understand open theism's possibilities, I found myself drawn to it. On my score, God was either limited by some sort of built-in constraint or limited Himself voluntarily. Constrained limitation meant God's limitations were *necessary* for some logical reason such as human free will. We are not determined puppets on a chain. Consequently, this free will capacity given to humans thus constrains what God *can* do. This worked well for developing the human responsibility aspect of my work with the environment. However, another logical reason, taken up extensively by Oord, was that of God's nature as being primarily love, thus requiring limitation. Voluntary limitation, on the other hand, means that God does not *have* to be self-limited but has choice in the matter. Oords' later work in uncontrolling love and essential kenosis reveals the difficulties of this self-limiting view.

Once again, I finished my program of study. Within a year, I had a wonderful opportunity to publish my dissertation. Elated, I approached my advisor with the news, but unfortunately we had a falling-out over religion, which pained me heavily. In spite of the conflict, the dissertation was published. Intensely distressed by the sore encounter, my throat was severely constricted, and I knew something needed to change.

God's uncontrolling love is connected to our deepest places, our deepest moments, and to our deepest desires. Feeling that I had always wanted to write a book on Heidegger, and feeling strengthened by just the thought of it, I drafted a paper which ended up getting me into yet another graduate program at another university to study again. I flourished, as reading Heidegger nourished me intellectually, bringing me joy and purpose. I never tired of his thought, of pondering the revealing nature of ideas, nature, truth, and reality. I recalled, though, that he was always to be on the back burner, with Christ in the driver's seat for my life.

Finally, with yet another graduate degree in hand and a published book on Heidegger, there were classes to teach, and places to go. We went first to Colorado where I carried a heavy load of adjunct teaching. We had fallen on hard times financially, in our ministry, and in our family. Not long after, we moved to a desert town in Arizona, where I taught philosophy at a local community college for a year. Seeing philosophy profoundly mean something to my students was deeply gratifying. Then, it seemed too good to be true—I landed my first full time faculty job at a brand new start-up university campus! The day I walked out of the interview for the job, everything that we had discussed fit so well with who I was and what I had to offer. That was the second time that I felt that God knew my name. With gusto, the pioneer spirit of launching a new school took hold, and there was much to do. At last, my whole academic portfolio was going to be used for a teaching career. Life had come full circle, and it was good. But, life is relentlessly moving on and, with it, heartaches come and go.

My divorce was one of them. It couldn't happen to me, but it did. After 34 years of life together, our marriage ended. Like the sudden Pacman "game over" pronouncement, it was too late. It all happened so fast, and there was nothing I could do to fix it. Somehow life had turned a corner. Yet another soul searching time of sadness for me ensued. Rejection and loss were expressed in the many journals that I wrote. I was alienated from church and friends, scrambling to find a place to be.

One exception, however, was a loyal and faithful church friend, Pam, who never let go of me. She met with me regularly, listening, coaching, and encouraging me in the Lord. She was like the coming of Titus, who was sent by God to comfort the believers. Where others seemed to avoid me, she went out of her way to check up on me. A godly person she was, who said she was praying for me. No doubt those prayers turned into action, because she amazingly hung on when many seemed not to care or did not know how to reach out in this situation. She seemed to know right where I was at, and she didn't balk at the challenges of aiding me. As I found out, transitioning from one reality to another is hard without support. Fortunately, God prompted Pam to accompany me in my intermediate, vulnerable zone between two realities and to help me attach properly to the other side. Fortunately, Pam listened to these promptings.

Thankfully, my dad also helped me figure out my housing and finances, even though he lived far away. This was very meaningful to me. Unfortunately, shortly thereafter, my mother was tragically in a car accident and struggled to survive for 68 days, before dying. She was a lovely Christian woman and it made no sense whatsoever for her life to end in such a state as that. We were stunned by the disaster and horrified by the seeming futility of it. The brutal destruction of her life had a jarring impact on all who knew her and loved her.

My studies of open theism and knowing that I could not blame God for this tragedy helped at a time such as this. Thank goodness I didn't belong to a church with a theology that said, "Everything happens for a reason," or, "it was her time to go," or, "this was part of God's plan for her." Clichés about God's ways being higher than ours would have been disturbing. Thankfully, no one was preaching the common Christian radio message: "God did this because you needed to learn something."

Open theism doesn't teach that God is in control, ordaining everything that occurs. Instead, God is experiencing time and reality, just as we are, and He hurts and agonizes with us in our hours of distress. Since my studies primarily came from a position of human free will constraining and limiting God, I was looking for answers in understanding the situation of my mother's death from that vantage point. In my rationality, I saw that free will could explain the tragedy of the twenty-one year old guy who was speeding and texting of his own volition when he destroyed my mother's life. But free will arguments alone cannot pacify the pain or bring a sense of the justice of God to my mom. They also do not provide an intimate connection with God, which is what was needed during this incident. For me, a more powerful reason than free will arguments had to come into play. And that's where God's uncontrolling love fit. Isaiah 63:9 expresses it well: "In all their affliction, He was afflicted." The stage upon which I was to understand God's love was the world of the accident, or any episode that I encounter. Seeing how His love was to be self-giving was yet to be known and experienced.

The aftermath of these two events, the divorce and the accident, were like the contents of a glass, the pieces of my life, being dumped out and strewn haphazardly across a table top. Scattered and tossed about, parts of me felt disjointed and undone. Yet there was still, remarkably, my center with God. There was nothing to do but to be and let be, wait it out, pick up the pieces, put one foot in front of the other, trust the Lord, and go on anyhow until time healed things. Some days were very hard...

It's funny how things happen, which really are not that funny at the time but in retrospect are amusing. In the depths of the saddest places of my life, guess what showed up again? A group of international Heideggerians found me! As I was in the throes of great grief, the first person who contacted me had read my book on Heidegger and wanted to do some writing with me. That was such an uplifting experience! We presented at a conference and found two other like-minded scholars who also became our good buds for the next three years, running around to conferences, speaking, writing, and Skyping. What more could I ask of life? Having someone to talk to about the things that really matter to me and to challenge my thinking—well, it was too good to be true. Having that connection was one of the ways I felt God loving me. I feel that God shares my deepest passions with me, and it tugs on my heart strings whenever He shows up in the intimate depths of my experience along with the profoundest meanings that I love, and that, for me, is uncontrolling love.

The four of us avid Heideggerians sat high over the city of San Antonio in the tower restaurant after speaking for a conference. The sun was going down, and the question was raised of how we all came to know and love Heidegger's work. Each shared their story. There was a certain sacredness in sharing my story with them, as I knew I would also be sharing my faith, something not shared with them before. After telling my story, one wistfully remarked that for me, the encounter with Heidegger had certainly been a life changing experience, and I wondered if they also sensed their own significance in my life and the presence of God with us.

Another curious event surprised me. On the home front, I had been praying for a place to serve God rather than sitting on the sidelines. In looking for another church at which to worship, I happened upon a congregation needing a minister of music. Leading choirs and praise band turned out to be a wonderful ministry! In addition, the pastor was also very gracious toward women in ministry and allowed me to preach whenever he was gone. This was an opportunity to see if I had gifts and graces for a preaching ministry. The Lord continues to bless my efforts in that capacity, and I have served there now for three years!

God's uncontrolling love also shows up in unfamiliar places. Last summer, I took a group of university students to Ecuador on a study abroad trip. The program provider, a Venezuelan educator who had fled his country under the recent duress, was accompanying us on our travels. Imagine my delight when I discovered that he had done his thesis on Heidegger and the agricultural system of Venezuela. How stimulating it was to share our mutual interests. It is quite rare to find people who share the same love for Heideggerian philosophy, and what an unusual meeting place of minds! Because of our common interests, I was able to also share my faith with him. Upon returning to the United States, we kept in contact, as a series of problems were facing him. Once, when it got very difficult, I urged him to visit the local Nazarene Church and told him that

God would meet him there. God did meet him there as an old friend recognized him, and by the end of the service prayed with him to give the Lord everything. My friend's life began to improve, and opportunities began to emerge as he sought God. I am reminded that the things we deeply care about, and on which we are able to connect deeply with others, are spaces where God deeply connects, as well.

Pursuing the writing of this essay and revisiting my past experiences has caused me to question whether the call on my life for a preaching ministry could yet be fulfilled. I made an appointment with the local Nazarene woman pastor, just to make some inquiries about the process of pursuing ordination at this juncture. She fairly rose from her seat with great enthusiasm at the news of my interest, and took me under her wing, so to speak, facilitating me to knock on that door again. Although much remains to be seen, a couple of preliminary steps have already shown hope. When deep calls to deep, we have a choice to answer the call. God lets us choose and works with our choices.

Sharon R. Harvey is the founding faculty member of the newest Arizona State University location at ASU Colleges of Lake Havasu City, Arizona. She directs the General Education program and teaches religion, philosophy and sustainability courses. Her research interests include Heideggerian eco-phenomenology, phenomenological education, and religion and the environment.

Essentially Uncontrolled Church
By Silas Krabbe

In walked Angel; slender in figure, average in height, quiet in footstep, with long dark hair and large brown eyes. We all shuffled, turned our heads, said "hello," welcomed her to the back row of chairs, and returned to the discussion we were having about the day's lectionary text, Amos 5:18-24:

> *Alas for you who desire the day of the LORD!*
> *Why do you want the day of the LORD?*
> *It is darkness, not light;*
> *as if someone fled from a lion,*
> *and was met by a bear;*
> *or went into the house and rested a hand against the wall,*

and was bitten by a snake.

Is not the day of the LORD *darkness, not light,*
and gloom with no brightness in it?
I hate, I despise your festivals,
* and I take no delight in your solemn assemblies.*
Even though you offer me your burnt offerings and grain offerings,
I will not accept them;
and the offerings of well-being of your fatted animals
I will not look upon.
Take away from me the noise of your songs;
I will not listen to the melody of your harps.
But let justice roll down like waters,
and righteousness like an ever-flowing stream.

I was pleasantly surprised that Angel had returned. She had stopped in soon after I had opened the door that Sunday afternoon. She had asked when the service was, and I told her that we usually began the service around three, but we had just put the coffee on and she was welcome to join us for a cup of coffee and some snacks. She congenially declined and slipped back out the door. It was a common interaction, and I thought nothing more about it.

When Angel had not returned by the time we began our service, sometime around three fifteen, I assumed she had found something else to do, or she had become distracted by an interaction out on the street.

We were in the midst of our discussion about the text from Amos when she came back. I was trying to show our community the self-critical mirror that Amos is holding up to the people of Israel in this text, as he confronts them with their lust for the destruction of their enemies. By turning the Day of the Lord against Israel; Amos holds up for examination the desire for violence within the people of Israel, which is not covered over by their self-righteous piety.

Ours is a discussion-based sermon style, wherein non-rhetorical questions are posed, answers are given, and conversation ensues. The connections made in conversation are not always as clearly linked as those in formal logical sequences or three part sermons. But it is far more welcoming and participatory for those who have been told for most of their lives that they are not smart enough to understand a sermon or a lecture, one put forward from a position of patriarchal power over the listener or dumbed down to such an extent the wisdom offered is so cliche it no longer has relevance to real life situations.

Somewhere in the midst of discussing the imagery of fleeing a lion and being met by a bear, and finding darkness not light in the day of judgement, Angel began to share. Her story poured out of her, like a dam had been breached: addiction, abuse, fear, loneliness, and alienation.

We sat. We listened. We gave space.

As the wave of words began to flow in a steadier and less rushed fashion, the stream of her thoughts began form a recognizable flow, recounting a story of violence wherein she found herself alone on a busy street being beaten and robbed, and as she tried to get away she was pepper sprayed in the face. Blinded, she recounted how she had been running down the middle of the street screaming for someone to help her, yet no one moved; no one offered her aid. She turned the question toward us: Why had no one helped? Why did no one offer assistance?

Some questions seem to have no immediate answers when asked. To answer too quickly can re-offend. The wisdom of listening and letting a question breathe can be its own beginning of healing.

As we sat and listened to Angel recount her experience of abandonment even in the midst of the crowd, we were shown a mirror—a mirror of our own apathy, comfort and inaction in the face of such injustice.

I could never have explicated the text in such a way as to communicate the vitriol and the verve with which Amos spoke against Israel, nor would my teaching have taught those present about the unbounded flows that are necessary to move in the ways of justice. It took Amos, sitting amongst us, to show us a mirror that reflected our own apathy, comfort, and inaction back to us through Angel's story.

Our discussion had been interrupted, overtaken, and it was for the better. The uncontrolled conversation that we held open, offered room for Angel to speak her piece. Little did we know or expect that Angel's story was the piece we needed to hear.

What would an uncontrolling ecclesiology—a theology of an uncontrolled church—be; what would it look like? If God is uncontrolling in relation to creation because of the shape of love, as demonstrated and defined by God, what does it mean to be a participant in the bride of Christ—the church? What does it mean to shape church order and structures to be an expression of this uncontrolling love? Where is the line between consistency of loving character and control as it relates to church expression? These are but a few of the ecclesiological questions that arise from the theological work Thomas J. Oord has done in expressing his position of essential kenosis, which requires further theological reflection, experimentation, and practice.[1]

Ours was a circuitous route toward an uncontrolled expression of belonging, participation, and being the church. Our teachers were not theologians from famed academic institutions, but individuals living in the alleyways behind the church buildings, whose presence and articulated desires taught us about the shape of love and its uncontrolling nature. So when reading Oord's theological works of love, we found a resonant chord that articulates the theological symphony already playing out in our midst.

Our church community was birthed out of the back door of a physical church; when a then youth pastor broke from his job description, compelled to spend a significant portion of his time connecting with the population that lived just beyond his office door in the alleyways of Vancouver. Out of those initial interactions, distributions of food hampers, and eventual relationships; he began an evening worship service to welcome in those who lived behind the church. From the church's

---

[1] See Thomas Jay Oord, *The Uncontrolling Love of God: An Open and Relational Account of Providence* (Downers Grove: InterVarsity Press, 2016).

conception, he attempted to subvert the established powered dynamics of 'ministering to' or 'providing service for' this population. Instead, the alleyway population would become the center of the church—its leaders and its members. Those with positions of social power in majority society were also welcome to join, that is if they were willing to engage in mutually transformative relationships by taking on a posture of humility toward the other expressed in the saying: "I need this other person in my life more than they need me."

From its origins as an evening service, the church moved into its own building; occupying an apartment style loft within a warehouse. Couches and tables were added, meals were served, and regular worship services were held on Saturday evenings and subsequently Sunday afternoons. Throughout this time we were learning, deconstructing, and slowly being released from our idol of control. The things we thought were important became less so, the need for fixed routines began to erode, and people with all their messy humanity became an embodied unit that formed the service. Sermons ended with a question period, services were disrupted by immediate pressing needs, and our Indigenous participants reminded us continually that time serves the people rather than the people serving the clock. After a series of unfortunate events with our landlord, we found a new home in an old church basement. Here too we learned that the space serves the community, not the other way around—the kitchen is in the basement, it's where nourishment resides.

What is the shape of love, of love reflected in the church? Is it like a plastic box with which you make sand castles? Simply filling it, turning it over, and slamming it down until there are identical replicas of little boxes all in a row? Or is the shape of love more like a hand that pats and shapes the sand into always-new configurations?

We're not as ingenious and creative as we might like to think. Poverty and marginalization have been our instructors instead of lavish offices providing theological high ground. We have never had the budget, or the numbers, to have a children's Sunday school; instructors, rooms, and resources are luxuries. So Sara and Michael sit at the same table with a box of construction paper, coloured pencils, scissors, and glue in-between them.

Sara is two, Michael is thirty-two; and contrary to what you may be conjuring in your imagination, Michael is not tasked with taking care of Sara during the service, nor in fact are they related. Rather both are often engaged in their own unique and independent art projects throughout the course of the service. The table sits in the middle of the basement; other tables and random chairs are pulled out and set up as people arrive. People are neither required to stand nor sit at certain times during the service, so Michael is able to listen, sing, and work on an art project all at once or in succession. As a former engineer, Michael knows a thing or two about order, sequence, and form, but as he sits in front of a box of construction paper those things find a place within the art and the experience but do not dictate the terms by which Michael must engage. Sara, on the other hand, also does not have to sit or stand on command, instead she is able to come and go freely as the art project captures her imagination, or not. Occasionally a ball or a guitar is far more interesting than the construction paper, and Sara will explore her surroundings as she sees fit. Our community, so often void of the joy of children due to socio-economic limitations, is free to revel in the freedom Sara displays. Children are rarities in our community as our context of urban poverty, addiction, and mental illness are barriers to having children, and those born in the neighbourhood are often scooped up and sent away into the foster care system that is governed by a European-settler understanding of what a family structure ought to look like. The church I grew up in also shipped the children away, down into the basement during the service. Here, we all meet in the basement, hearing from and seeing everyone together in whatever ways they choose to participate that day. Sara belongs. Sara belongs *in* the community and belongs *to* the community. It is here, between the pillars and the walkers, she took her first steps; it is here she is free to meltdown without condemnation; it is here she can run forward and change the tune of her father's guitar or bang on a drum alongside her mother.

While Sara and Michael are the regulars who are seated by the box of art supplies, they are often joined by an assortment of people from our community who either enjoy watching them create pieces of art or who want to join in their own way. Here we do not just say everyone is welcome to engage in their own way; we demonstrate it to one another every week in regular ways. Joining in our own way, as demonstrated by Sara and Michael, enables others to freely express themselves in the service as well: standing, sitting, leaving to smoke a cigarette, getting a third of fourth cup of coffee, or even sleeping through the afternoon if the coffee is ineffective. The space retains a buzz throughout the service, as people come and go, say hello, and attend to the needs of our bodies.

Far too often, we default to engineering our services rather than creatively playing in their poetry.

Time is money; so the colloquial saying goes. And if the love of money is the root of all kinds of evil, then was does that say about our love of time?[2] Ordered time, controlled time...

Joe came in angry. That much was clear. One look at his face and it was evident that he was hurt, angry, and ready to lash out.

While the intensity of his anger was obvious, the needed response to such transparency is a murky business. I took it slow.

After Joe had poured a cup of coffee and made himself a peanut butter and jam sandwich—elements that occasionally have healing power—I walked over to Joe and asked him how his week had been. Then I got it.

I had only known Joe for a few weeks. He had told me some stories, many of which had seemed fanciful, and after having spent a number of years in a community where over 60% of the population has an open mental health case file, I had learned to just roll with it and try to piece together the narrative of the other's life over the course of many cups of coffee. I have also learned in my context the importance of

---

[2] See I Timothy 6:10

delaying judgments of veracity, because many of the people with whom I regularly interact have lived lives that seem unbelievable because their experiences are so far removed from my own. Joe was one of those people on whom I had been reserving judgment, because I found myself skeptical of many of his stories, but confronting him about their authenticity seemed like a foolish endeavour on my part.

On this day, however, it did not matter if I listened or not. Joe was going to give me a piece of his mind. What ensued can only be described as a verbal berating, as I became the target for all of Joe's anger, frustrations, and hurt. It was not the first time that I, as a white, middle-class, male, served as the archetype upon which to cast the blame for all of the hurtful experiences perpetrated by people who look like me, and I can assure you it will not be the last. From colonialism, to foster care, to police brutality and the ineffectiveness of the western legal system: I personify them all. As it turned out, Joe was emotionally processing his children being taken into the foster care system and was understandably angry, hurt, and feeling helpless in confronting the monolith that is the Ministry of Children and Family Services and the western legal system.

In an attempt to defuse the situation, I was able to direct Joe to the doorway where I would listen to him, without it being right in front of the coffee pot where everyone else was hanging out, as anger and aggression can trigger so many other members of our community whose own pasts have been shaped by violent and aggressive encounters. He continued to yell, shout, and blame me for my ineffectiveness in preventing things from happening to his family. After about half an hour

I told him I had to set up for the service but he was welcome to stay, and stay he did.

He sat steaming in the back of the group as we sang some songs and prayed. Once we got to the discussion time of our gathering, we read the passage and after I asked the first question, Joe found his platform from which to speak. And speak he did: to the whole community with a continuous stream of thoughts. There was no stopping his five to ten minute soliloquy. We heard his grievances and all the reasons he felt he deserved respect from the system that had harmed him. Catching a lull in his speaking I reaffirmed, pivoted, and redirected us to the passage we had read. Joe was content. He had said his piece to the community. No one told him he had to stop speaking; no one told him he was out of line. Instead, we bent, morphed, and adapted our community so that Joe in his current shape would fit.

Now, after having been part of our faith community for over two years, Joe has been able to thank the community during our discussion times for being a place in which he has felt heard, supported, and where he belongs. He still on occasion will rail against society regarding the harms and disrespect it has shown him. But he has a place—a place in which to be heard, and he has in his own way communicated that he receives that place, the space and time in which to speak as an act of love, which calms him down, re-centers him, and enables him to try to get through another week. Such is the persistence, and empowerment, of an uncontrolling yet stubbornly resolved love. Jane in turn has thanked Joe for his presence with us. There is a peculiar reciprocity and gratitude that uncontrolled time can cultivate.

Jane is a highly efficient and effective human resources negotiator for a major organization in our city. Her days are often filled to bursting with the number of tasks she is required to accomplish as well as the stress of taking on high-stakes employment negotiations. Hers is a world of efficiency, tasks, and outcomes. Mosaic, the gathering of our faith community, is the time in her life in which she is able to shed some of those priorities of efficiency and, instead, favour focusing on developing compassion and empathy. Joe's outbursts, interruptions, and claim on community time are the deconstructive forces that enable the dismantling of an efficiency, hyper-productive, and reductionist mindset that diminishes the person to the problem they represent.

Subsequent to Jane's initial acceptance that she needs Joe, more than Joe needs her, she has told us that she is challenged to actively listen to Joe rather than merely wishing he would stop talking. It is a practice of love in the midst of the slow-motion messiness of lived reality instead of the corporate control of streamlined rigidity. Our time together becomes our teacher, when we give up control of it and let it serve the other.

If God is uncontrolling, might we necessarily need to change the structure of our interactions in order for the people, spaces, and times to be formed by love? Is there room in our churches for people like Angel, spaces for Sara and Michael, and enough time for Joe to be heard? Or do our gods of image, structure, and order prevent us from being love to those who are essentially uncontrolled? Furthermore, if a controlling interaction is not reflective of the love shown to us by God, then how might that alter our understanding of tough love, which is often invoked to maintain a status quo, an image, or 'divinely given' order of things? If we follow after an uncontrolling God, then I think we are just beginning to explore what this might mean for our churches as they respond uniquely to their own uncontrolled contexts!

Silas Krabbe is the Community Theologian and Coordinator at Mosaic Church located in Vancouver's downtown eastside, one of Canada's poorest neighborhoods. A graduate of Columbia Bible College (BA in Biblical Studies and Community Development) and Regent College (MATS in Christianity and Culture), he seeks to entangle contemporary theologies issued from the ivory tower with back-alley musings about the world.

Is Love Enough
Wendy Breningstall-Ismael

I Met My Husband at the Airport

People say that when they go to pick up their spouse after a long journey or when they are the one coming home, but I *literally* met my husband at the airport—my husband, Mohammed. When I meet a new friend and begin to share our life story... and our love story... the looks I receive are priceless. There is usually an awkward silence, as if I am joking. They wait for the punch line, but there is none. I met my Muslim husband at the airport, and I kinda love that part!

Why? Because it was during the time when people were suspicious of Muslims on airplanes. Maybe that is still the case, but not as much as it was then.

I had avoided flying to New York City for almost two years, even though my friend who lived there kept asking me to come. Her husband had a friend who wanted to meet me. He often asked to speak with me on the phone, and by 'often,' I mean several times per week. I always said no. I didn't know him. Why would I want to talk with him? One day, he got on the line, anyway. He said hello, and I panicked. I didn't know what to say, so I hung up! This was my first reaction to the man who would one day be my husband. That was the first year.

Over the next ten months, my friend continued to ask me to visit, but the timing was never right… or maybe I was just lazy. It wasn't that I didn't want to go, but making a trip to New York seemed like a lot of work. Finally, she came to visit me. As we were having coffee one morning, she said, "I miss having you around! Come back with me for a few weeks. The flight is already covered!"

Well, what excuse did I have now? There was nothing keeping me from making the trip. At most, I would have a two week vacation, and then I would return to my life as it was. I couldn't come up with a good excuse to refuse such an offer, so I made a split second decision and found myself on a plane, heading toward a city against which I was prejudiced, wondering if I might freeze to death or be eaten by a rat or a cockroach!

When we landed, my friend's husband was there along with this man whom I had never met… whom I had hung up on… who had clearly stated that he would one day marry me, which is either sweet or creepy, depending on your point of view! He knew so little about me, but his interest was piqued from a photo and a description of the 'good church girl' that I was. It's rather incredible that his first impression of me was that he liked me immediately, because I gave him a chance… because I wasn't afraid. It's funny, because although it is true, I am also very shy, and I had absolutely nothing to say to him at first, other than a polite, "hello."

I don't think I'm rude, but there I was, standing in an airport in Queens, white and female and statistically (wrong or not) more vulnerable than powerful or frightening, awkwardly greeting a man of whom many people were inappropriately afraid to such a degree that he was not even introduced to me with his real name but as "Samir," which I guess is less common and less frightening to most. And it is *part* of his name, unlike the farce of a nametag he was once required to wear at work, declaring him, "Malcolm." How is that helpful? I knew his religion, and I knew his name, so I asked him what I should call him. I would learn later that he appreciated that greatly, because I didn't treat him as less or run away. I never acted as if this alone was a reason to be afraid of him or to act like he was going to commit a crime. He knew immediately that he did not have to pretend to be anyone but himself with me.

But it's one thing to exchange pleasantries at the airport. It's quite another to actually get to know someone. Mohammed was a housemate of my friend and her husband, and now I was a guest in the same house. There were also two other couples who joined us, to show me the sights of New York, so Mohammed and I naturally were often grouped together. I'm pretty sure this was planned! We would sit together at dinner, and then when the others had gone to their homes and my friend and her husband would turn in for the night, only the two of us were left. We would sit in the living room watching TV, and there were times when I wondered whether or not I should retreat to my room, but I really didn't want to hide. After all, the living room was for everybody, and he was doing nothing to scare me off. So we sat... in silence... night after night, until one or the other got too tired and went to bed. I consider myself a friendly person, if shy, but I just didn't know what to say.

Slowly, things began to shift and change. One night we were all at the mall, at the food court, eating pretzels and getting ready to see a movie. When I came back from the bathroom, there was a big, white, blushing teddy bear waiting for me. Mohammed told me that some random guy at the mall happened to think I was cute and dropped it off. Turns out he was funny, and I totally played along. The next gift was a DVD, which broke up our nightly TV time a little bit. And somehow during this time I fell for him.

What is a "Good Church Girl" doing with a Muslim Husband?

As a white Christian growing up in the US, discrimination is not something I dealt with often. Oddly, putting into words the discrimination we have experienced is the hardest part, but perhaps not for the reasons most people would assume. I remember getting upset over things... not understanding... venting... but it's difficult to remember specific events. After so many years, these things feel like they happened a lifetime ago. It hurt when 'friends' talked about me derogatively, behind my back. Many of them vanished when I got married, but it can be difficult to determine how much of that was discrimination and how much of it was just what happens to everyone. Of course, I am certainly better off without some of them in my life, anyway.

Something that stung deeply was the notion that Mohammed married me for the sole purpose of attaining a green card! Let's just say he did. That isn't the most practical way, by far. He wasn't granted US citizenship until we had been married for eight years. That's a long time to be in a sham marriage!

The path to citizenship is long and hard. I have never had to prove my love for this country, but my husband has. He has been fingerprinted, background checked, and passed a citizenship test that I honestly doubt I could pass, myself. We endured this time consuming, very expensive, invasive process together, and to question to truth of our love is deplorable.

It hurt at another deep level when people began to question my faith, assuming I would have to convert to Islam. There are plenty of things that have caused me to have doubts—sickness and suffering, hate, death—but my husband's religion has never been one of them. Some of the questions that were leveled at me were just a matter of curiosity, but others were more than that. Realistically, some were just strange: "Does he make you walk behind him?" Uh… no.

I did, of my own accord, decide to cover my hair as an act of support for my husband, for a period of time. I didn't change religions. It was still me. But, I was fully committed to it, and it made for some interesting and horrible interactions (which is sort of hypocritical if you think about the Christian Scriptures that encourage women to cover their heads). I was working as a cashier at the time, and I was shocked when someone who didn't like a store return policy referred to me as, "you stupid foreigner."

I'm decent at ignoring rude customer comments, but before I knew it, something came out of my mouth, this time: "I was born here."

She replied, "Well obviously you don't know our way of life." Then she threw the items at me and left.

During this period of time, I was also called a terrorist in a variety of public places. Admittedly, there were some other interactions that were somewhat humorous, as confused people asked whether I was Muslim, Jewish, Mennonite, or Amish! I covered my hair, but I'm still Christian! Religion isn't really about this kind of thing, at all, which serves to underscore the point that people have been terribly confused about the differences among categories such as race, religion, and customs. Some have expressed concern about my son, wondering how it works for him to be "part Muslim." I think they must certainly mean "part Arabic," but explaining the difference to those who simply don't get it is a challenge.

Even beyond all of this is the peculiar behavior of people who are friendly to us, because they know us personally, but who continue to say discriminatory things in our presence. Talk of deportation can be terrifying. When people we know say, "Muslims should not be allowed in the United States," or, "All Muslims should be deported," or, "The only good Muslim is a dead Muslim," I am taken aback. I want to ask, "Did you mean everyone except the Muslim I'm married to?" That doesn't make it any better, though, and I don't really know how I should take any of this. We are fortunate to not live in fear of actual deportation, but I am left wondering if even those who talk with us casually would prefer to deport my husband, if they could. And what about my American-born son, with all of this confusion about race and religion? Do they see him as a threat, because he has Arabic blood flowing through his veins? Would they honestly take him from me, given the chance? Would they just go ahead and deport me, too? I would like to think it's all talk, and they would not actually support such a thing. Mostly, I think the interactions that lead to these questions inside of me have been stupid, flippant comments, but maybe we should be more careful with our words, because contrary to the nursery rhyme, they do have the power to break us.

Love Works for Us. That's What Matters.

Mohammed and I are vastly different people in so many ways, but that's not all that unusual in marriage. He's more structured, neat. My work space is organized chaos. With our son, though… I'm the 'bad cop.' I think a lot of moms can relate to that! Meals are always funny. I'm not sure we ever eat the same thing. This is the mundane way of our everyday life. People ask what it's like to be married to a Muslim, and the question seems somehow 'off' to me. I don't know any other way. I would imagine it's about the same as anyone else whose husband likes meat and rice, while she would prefer a good yogurt! Love works for us, and that's what matters.

Realistically, it would be more difficult for me to be married to an atheist. Faith is important to both of us, so we understand one another in this way. We celebrate both Christian and Muslim holidays. We go to both mosque and church. Rather than lessen my faith, it makes it stronger. I sometimes wonder what is wrong with learning about another way? People want to put God in a box or exercise some sort of control over God, but I can feel God in a church or by the lake, and it isn't as if God isn't allowed in the mosque. I'm good wherever I go! Interestingly, even though we practice different religions, we have many of the same questions. I pray to God to guide us both.

I've come to a realization. I truly thought facts and love would be enough. But you can't reason with bigots, and they speak the loudest. You can't reason with liars. You can't reason with people that hate. You can't reason with people that have no empathy… This is the hardest lesson on humanity. But luckily most people aren't like this.

Wendy Breningstall-Ismael was born and raised in Michigan and currently resides in New York with her husband and their one son, who is trying his hardest to make her into a runner. She likes to read when she has time, anywhere and anything, including the back of the cereal box.

Friend Divorce
Emma Elias

I f we have any desire to live into the life of Jesus, if Jesus is God, and if God is love… If love is uncontrolling, then we cannot exercise control over the people who flow into and out of our lives, even if it hurts to let go.

Disengagement

Some time ago, one of my favorite colleagues, friends, and overall people (hereby referred to as [Redacted 1]) broke up with me. There was no romantic relationship involved, so I recognize this language is controversial. I chose to use it, because that night made me feel a whole lot like the time in eighth grade when Pete Houston dumped me, in part so he could be amusement park field trip riding partners with one of my best friends.[1] I cried both times.

Pete surely realized that he needed to pair with someone else if he wanted to ride roller coasters. [Redacted 1], though… he wanted to get off the ride. In some ways, I understand. We had been on one heck of a figurative roller coaster for too long.

If you're looking for a scandal, however, you have come to the wrong place. There is no scandal. Try not to be too disappointed. Even so, this can't stop other people from thinking what they'll think, and sometimes those perceptions make our choices for us. The more I've pondered this, the clearer it has seemed to me. Of course, my perception isn't perfect either, but the end result is a matter of facts and figures.

After several years of close friendship—in the middle of the night, via social media messages—we disengaged, because that's what he wanted. When someone asks you to disengage, you only have two choices. You can do it, or you can become a stalker. I am no stalker. I disengaged immediately.

Within the intricate concepts of free agency, choice, and control lies an unfair component. As it turns out, unchecked free agency may be used by others to force us into (or out of) situations, without our consent. We are not actually free to do, be, or have whatever we want, because structures of power and control ensure that someone else might thwart our plans at any moment. I used to think God exercised that kind of

---

[1] This name has been changed for the protection of middle school romance.

control, but I've changed my mind, because love cannot possibly hurt like this.

Dissolution of a desired relationship naturally causes some degree of sadness and the need for appropriate processing, but there were other connected issues I did not expect to encounter. I legitimately thought that night was going to be the worst of it, but then I remembered we run in all the same circles with all the same people. We could commit to never communicating with one another again, but that wouldn't stop our mutual friends from creating interaction between us.

Who Gets the "Kids?"

Thankfully, I have never been involved in a custody battle; but I have many friends who have, and they attest to the horror of suddenly having their children with them only half the time—or not at all. As a mother, I fully understand that *this* does not compare equally to *that*, but it's the best parallel I have for the purpose of this narrative.

[Redacted 1] and I have so many mutual acquaintances, and the number keeps growing. When this all went down, I naively wondered how we might split them up. In hindsight, that was ridiculous. I'm an introvert. He's an extrovert. He gets to keep (most of) the friends. As if that wasn't bad enough, you may or may not be familiar with the social construct that allows introverts a seat at tables of conversation, *if* they bring an extrovert along. It took me awhile to recognize what a blow it was to not only lose a large chunk of community but to lose *my* extrovert!

My voice didn't rebound for months, and when it did, it didn't sound quite like me.

But there was one friend (hereby referred to as [Redacted 2]) I worried about more than the rest, because almost all of our conversation had been communal in nature. With just about everyone else, there was no awkward pause—at least not more awkward than usual. I'm not sure most people suspected anything was amiss, at all. But with [Redacted 2], it was necessarily different, because the dynamics changed completely.

I hated that. I think the hardest part about it was that I had no desire to recount the story to [Redacted 2], so I didn't. Instead, I just pulled back with no explanation at all, dropping a one liner here or there so as not to be rude but essentially losing that second relationship, as well, because so much silence was required. If it's difficult to lose one of your favorite people, it's even worse to lose two.

But wait, there's more…

Standing Alone in a Crowded Room
(AKA: What I Learned from Taylor Swift)[2]

You're going to have to take this next part with a grain of salt, because many T. Swift songs are about romance gone bad, but I've learned to sing them *all* out of context… loudly… (still no scandal).

Five months after we stopped communicating, I found myself in the same room with [Redacted 1]. I had prepared myself for how much it

---

[2] Swift, Taylor. Story of us. On *Speak Now*. Big Machine Records, LLC BTMSR0500A, 2010, compact disk.

Friend Divorce

was going to hurt to breathe the same air and not form words, if this day ever came (and it was inevitable—see: running in the same circles). At the point at which I was relatively sure the day had, indeed, come, I strategically chose to occupy space where I would neither be responsible for breaking silence nor excessively accessible.

[Redacted 1] sat down in my line of sight. Let's assume that was unintentional. When there was a break in the program, he approached me. Let's assume that was not. Again, free agency and power structures rear their ugly heads here, because whoever utters the words, "Let's disengage," also has all of the ability to choose the terms of re-engagement.

After nearly half a year of silence, I wasn't sure how to react. I had *not* prepared myself for was how much it was going to hurt to make an attempt to talk about the weather, at arm's length. Introverts suck at small talk. I came to this moment with the assumption that the deafening silence was going to remain between us and around us and creeping into every inch of atmosphere, forever. Even though that was horrible; I could push through it, because it's what I expected.

I want to be very careful to make a distinction between what I expected and what I wanted. *None of this* is what I wanted, and perhaps that made it even more difficult to know what I should say. I stumbled over some sentences and choked back some tears.

Overall, it was awful.

Still, life goes on.

Me 2.0

I spent a pretty decent amount of time trying to figure out how to plug the gaping hole in my life that accompanied the loss of [Redacted 1]. The truth is he was filling a lot of roles for which other people are aptly qualified. It's been interesting, finding those people and holding on for dear life!

I've asked myself a lot of questions that sound something like this: "Who else meets the criteria to be one of my favorite colleagues, friends, and overall people?"

The answer to that question has often caught me by surprise, and I am incredibly happy with the many new relationships that have formed.

In this age of social media, however, there are some things that have been *too* hard for me to process. The greatest example comes in the form of watching my own replacement. I've started referring to her as "Me 2.0," because the other name I had for her is entirely inappropriate, and I legitimately like her.

I try to simply avoid their engagement, but sometimes I can't. I do hold onto the fact that there is only one real me. I feel unbearably confident that there are holes she can't fill; because I know with certainty there are some wounds in my own life that are going to continue to bleed, even if I make a thousand great connections. Sometimes that feels comforting, but mostly I wish it would just stop hurting. Honestly, sometimes I wish I was wrong. Sometimes I wish there really *was* a Me 2.0 and a [Redacted 1] 2.0 and a reasonable replacement part for every broken relationship.

Friend Divorce

Things are Getting Better

I've moved from a place of overwhelming grief (this is no exaggeration) to a place of acceptance. I'm still not OK with not being friends, and I doubt I ever will be. But I also recognize that there's not much I can do about it, unless I actually *do* want to become a stalker… which I don't. There are definitely some things in my life that have suffered irreparable losses alongside the loss of [Redacted 1]. I miss collaborative writing. I hate that he didn't proofread this piece.

The other day, [Redacted 2] reached out, so there's that. I am starting to feel as if some semblance of a new normal could spring up with the mutual friends.

My next hope in all of this is that I will finally allow the residual sadness to just be. I've done a lot of hiding behind anger and sarcasm, but I think I'm moving to a place where I will simply allow myself to cry if I feel like it, and I hope I'm going to feel like it a lot less often.

It hasn't been easy, but I'm finding my voice apart from [Redacted 1]'s influence in my life. There are some things for which I will always be grateful to him, but friendship takes two, and it's time to let go.

Emma Elias is a pastor, freelance writer, and mom (not necessarily in that order). She lives in the Pacific Northwest, where she enjoys building castles and drawing lines in the sand. Someday she would like to visit the seven natural wonders of the world.

Don't Take Off Running
Ben Graham

While in high school, I realized that I was different from most of my male peers. I noticed that I didn't look at women like the rest of my friends. Instead, I started looking at men in different ways. I remember being a freshman in high school, having a girlfriend, and watching as one particular guy walked by us. I remember how he smelled so warm and earthy and how his eyes were a beautiful hazel color that shined in every light. It wasn't until my freshman year of college that I made peace with myself by admitting that I am, in fact, gay. This was very difficult because I was brought up in a religious household where I was told that God did not like homosexuals.

Throughout high school; I remember thinking to myself that I had to be straight, because only straight people go to Heaven. I believed this so much that I would not have anything to do with anyone who was a part of the LGBTQ+ community. Granted, my rural school was literally situated among four cornfields. There were a total of five 'out' people in the entire school community. Ironically, one was my girlfriend who was also my best friend. Looking back at it now, I guess this was the first hint I had.

Over the course of my teenage years, I fell more and more into denial about my sexual orientations. I remember a voice in my head constantly repeating, "I am gay" and it drove me crazy. I wasn't thinking it and I tried to get the voice to say, "I am straight." It did not really work. The voice turned that phrase into, "I am straight up gay." I think that was my second clue.

It took four long years to finally come to terms with my sexuality. I had a girlfriend at the time when I kissed my first man. I remember the day as if it were yesterday. I was sitting in a lounge with three of my friends, two of them were women and the third a gay man, and we were reciting a script for one of my female friend's class projects. The script required me to get a little physical with my male friend, so we were playfully rubbing each other's chests and arms. It was after I had rubbed his chest for a long time that a voice in my head said to kiss the guy. Being a young man with his first taste of freedom, I leaned in and kissed him. Both of my female friends freaked out, and the guy was dumbfounded. It was then that I realized I was gay. I felt more kissing this guy once than I had when I kissed my girlfriend. I like to think that voice in my head was God telling me to become comfortable with my sexuality.

As it turned out, the man I kissed would become my first boyfriend. He was Christian as well, so I thought it was a match made in Heaven. However, it turned out that it would be a very trying time for me. I kept my relationship and sexuality hidden from my parents for several months. It was a difficult time not only because of that but also due to the fact that my very religious boyfriend tried to break off our relationship several times; because his pastor had preached about the how homosexuality was one of the biggest sins. Throughout this, I refused to break up with him because he was my first love. I remember going to his church one Sunday. After the service, he and I were sitting in my car and he said, "I'm sorry, Ben, but I don't think God likes the fact I'm in a homosexual relationship." That's when I told him that I believed God loved everyone, despite their supposed sins.

That was not the only time my boyfriend and I almost broke up because of what his pastor had preached. Ultimately, I broke up with him in the end, but I had learned from that relationship that God loved everyone. I didn't let myself become bitter over the multiple times my boyfriend had tried to break up with me. Instead, I used each moment as proof to myself that I was gay and a Christian at the same time. These identities did not have to be mutually exclusive.

During the time that followed, I eventually told my parents about my homosexuality. My mom and her two sisters were pastor's kids, so all three of them know a lot about the Bible. It turned out my mom was the most religious out of the three. I had told everyone on both sides of my family, besides my grandparents, that I was gay and they were all very accepting, even my religious brother. I vividly remember the evening that I told my parents. My father, mother, and I were going to spend the night at one of my aunt's and uncle's houses in Michigan, because the next day we were walking in a Walk to End Alzheimer's (my grandma on my mom's side of the family had been diagnosed with Alzheimer's). I had told my aunt beforehand in a text message that I wanted to tell my parents. I was planning to tell them at the starting line and then take off running because I was afraid of what they were going to say or do. My aunt had a different plan.

My father, mother, aunt, uncle, and I were all sitting in the living room, having random discussions and conversations, when the room fell silent. It was then that my aunt said something to my parents, "So, Ben has something to tell you."

I almost got up and left the room, because I was so scared. Both of my parents sat in silence until I finally said, "Mom, Dad… I am gay…"

The first words out of my mom's mouth were, "I know, Ben."

I was so relieved until my mom finished what she was going to say, "And I'll pray for you."

The conversation quickly went south from there. It turned into an argument between my mom and my aunt that left both of them in tears. I turned to my dad, whom I had been told by his younger sister was a homophobe, and asked what he thought. He just shrugged his shoulders.

It was then that I knew if a supposed homophobe could accept me, God would accept me, too.

As for my mother, she eventually came around and supported me. She didn't let this moment turn her bitter either. She used this to grow spiritually, just as I had done. God did not cause any of this. All God had done was create me. Life did the rest. God's love is not contingent on sexual orientation, although people try to manipulate God's words. Why would a loving and just God say, "I love everyone so much that I will give up my only son in order to let everyone into my Kingdom," and then turn around to say that only heterosexual men and women are allowed into Heaven? It doesn't make any sense. God loves everyone the same amount, unconditionally.

Ben Graham was born and raised in Peru, Indiana. He has never been one for organized religion, but still believes in God and His power. Always struggling to find his own way to speak with God, Ben has become a more a spiritual Christian by following God's number one rule: Love thy neighbor the way you love thyself.

Desires of the Heart
Kara Rich

You can believe in the impossible. I knew what story I wanted to tell, but I didn't know how I was going to go about telling it. Each one of us has an idea about how we want things to go in our lives. We have prayer requests: We have hopes and dreams. We bring them to God, and we hope he's going to help us to accomplish these things, but we have a definite plan regarding how we want it to go down. It's like we, in our finite minds, take a pencil and a piece of paper and we start drawing out what we want to happen in our lives. We think our pictures are awesome! But God uses colors and dimensions we haven't even thought of.

I was raised as one of seven kids, my childhood was very happy, and our family was really close, so I started my pencil drawing there. I always knew… *knew*… I was going to be a mother. There was no doubt. I have always loved kids and preferred the company of kids to the company of adults! I only went to college because everybody expected me to go to college. I didn't have career dreams and goals, but I had my eye on the 'real prize,' getting married and having children.

When I met my husband, Phil, he had recently been saved and had started attending my church. I had never met anybody like him. He was incredibly dedicated and disciplined. We started to date, and as we got closer and began to consider spending a life together, he dropped a bombshell. Years before, he had had a vasectomy. That did not fit into my plan!

We looked into it and found that reversals can be successful, so I figured that must be God's plan for us. I clung to Psalm 37:4, and I was delighting myself in the Lord.[1] I was holding up my end of the bargain, so I figured God had to hold up his end, as well. He had to give me the desires of my heart, which were children.

We got married, and we decided to spend the first few years building a solid marriage. It was awesome. We had a lot of time together and a Harley Davidson! When we weren't riding (and we did a lot of riding), Phil was meticulously polishing that thing, and it was his baby. We had a lot of fun, and although I thoroughly enjoyed it, it was not *my* baby. The longings inside of me were stirred and growing, because my

---

[1] "Delight thyself also in the LORD: and he shall give thee the desires of thine heart" (KJV).

sisters were having babies, all my friends were having babies, everywhere I looked, people were having babies! It just seemed so easy for everybody.

So, I convinced Phil it was time for the reversal. We needed to get going! However, we found out that it was not covered by insurance, it was going to cost several thousand dollars, and we didn't have that kind of money. That was the first of many depressing blows. I thought, "OK, God, how can you do this to me? You see my drawing here. You know my hopes and dreams."

A lot of people around me didn't really know how I felt, because I always tried to put on a happy face regardless of what was going on. I don't like people to feel sorry for me, so I hid it as well as I could. I had nieces and nephews whom I really loved, but ultimately, when they were scared or wanted to be tucked in, they didn't want me. They wanted their moms. I cried a lot at night. I think Phil got tired of hearing it, and then one day he came into church late (which was unusual for him), and I asked him, "Why are you late?"

His response was, "I sold my Harley, so I can have the vasectomy reversal surgery."

Anyone who knew Phil at that time knows what a sacrifice that was, and I just thought, "OK. We're getting somewhere. My plan is going to come to pass."

The reversal was successful, and we were so excited, but months passed with no pregnancy. When we went back for a follow-up appointment, we were told our best hope would be in vitro fertilization. I felt like the room was swimming. It just sounded ugly to me. It was not what I wanted. I just wanted to have a baby the 'real' way. But I thought to myself, "The doctor said this is impossible, so clearly God is just going to do it, and the doctors are going to say, 'Wow! I don't know how this happened!'"

Thus began a vicious cycle. Every month, before I started my period, I would take a pregnancy test. I would actually go buy them at different places, because I thought people would think, "Oh, here comes that girl who thinks she's pregnant, every month." I even went out of town, sometimes, and I kept track of where I went. They were always negative, and I would just start praying for the next month.

One Wednesday night, when I was particularly down, I was attending a prayer meeting at our church, and they were singing, "What a Friend I have in Jesus," and I was just thinking, "Huh. God is not my friend, and I'm not singing."

My intent was to hurt God. I was thinking that God wasn't doing anything for me, so why should I sing? The next morning, I woke up and studied Scripture anyway, and it was as if God was audibly speaking to me, because his presence was so close, reminding me that he was with me all this time and that I did not lack anything. I needed to be reminded of the blessings in my life, and I began to write them in the margins of my Bible. I was running out of space! *God's* intent was *not* to hurt me, but even though I resolved to trust, I entered into another season of ups and downs, like a roller coaster!

About this time, a new doctor came to town. My mom worked at the hospital and she talked with him quite a bit and confided in him about my struggle. He got really excited, because he had recently gotten new equipment for artificial insemination, and he was itching to try it on somebody!

Again, I thought, "Oh! So *that's* how God is going to work out my plan! God won't let me down!" Back to Psalm 37:4.

Another cycle had just started, so I began the process of taking my temperature to determine when I was ovulating. I called and scheduled an appointment at the right time and spent about an hour hanging upside-down on a hospital bed. Then I went home and hung upside-down on my stairs. Month after month, when I went back in, I heard, "I'm sorry. It just didn't work." I cried every time. Sometimes my doctor even cried.

We did this for 18 months. After about a year, I was so tired, and I just cried out to God for him to tell me if this wasn't to be. I wanted to be able to get on with my life, to be able to think of something else. I pleaded for him to speak to me through Scripture. I just wanted to open up the Bible and hear a word from God, and I *do not* suggest this for anyone else. I don't ordinarily do this. This was the only time I have ever done this, but I was desperate. I opened up to II Kings, and I was like, "Thanks a lot, God. I'm sure there's nothing in here!"

But as I read, my attention was piqued by the story of Elisha and the Shunammite woman who had no children—who did, indeed, conceive and have a son "at this season."[2] I was excited to the point of shouting, because this surely must mean I would finally have a baby, but at the next doctor's appointment, I found it was still not to be.

Of course, then I kept changing what I thought the Scripture meant. Maybe it didn't mean 'this season,' as in nine months from now but this literal season, next year. That gave me (and God) a couple more months to play with. But as more time passed, there was still no baby.

Phil began to tell me that he thought I was putting God in a box, insisting in my own timing. I hated him for that. I thought he was crazy! I wasn't putting God in a box; I was believing him! What I failed to realize was that I was still selfishly clinging to my own perception of how life had to be in order for my dreams to be fulfilled. I wanted everything my way.

The more time that passed, the lower I was feeling. I dreaded Mother's Day at church, when all the mothers would stand and I had to sit, when all the mothers were given flowers and I walked out with nothing and felt empty inside, too. One Mother's Day, I walked out a little early in order to avoid going through that again, and I was sitting in my car, crying, when a little girl from my Sunday School class came out to me and motioned for me to roll down the window and handed me a flower, saying, "This is for you, because you're going to be a good mother someday." I have never forgotten that. God spoke to me through that little girl, who was willing to be God's voice.

---

[2] See II Kings 4

Phil eventually began to say things to me like, "Am I not enough?"

And I said, "Seriously?"

I looked into in vitro fertilization in Iowa City, which has the best program in the United States... right in our back yard! Phil wasn't for it, he knew it was going to be difficult and expensive, and he was happy with us the way we were, but he finally, reluctantly agreed.

I was pumped full of hormones, given as daily injections. I went to Des Moines every other day to monitor blood levels. The stress of the situation was enough to make me half crazy, but with the hormones on top of that, it just wasn't good. My family, and my church family and friends were such a great support during that time, and most people knew what we were going through and prayed a lot for us.

Well, the time came for the harvesting of the eggs, and the hormone levels were perfect, the doctors were really excited, and they told me that I was a really good candidate. They wanted to do a quick ultrasound before the surgery, and as I'm lying there the doctor says, "holy cow!" You never want to hear that. He went and got other people, and there was a big crowd at the end of my bed just gasping. Evidently, I was very fertile. Normally when women are given these hormones they'll produce maybe six or seven eggs, but I had forty. According to the doctor that was both good news and bad news. The good news was we were going to have a really good chance of fertilizing an egg. The bad news was there was a rare chance that I would experience ovarian hyperstimulation, which is very dangerous but occurs in less than 0.01% of patients. They were able to harvest fifteen good eggs, which would give us three tries, implanting five per try. After the first try, things looked good.

I went to Des Moines two days later to have my labs monitored, but I didn't feel well. By the time we got there, Phil had to put me in a wheelchair to get me to the lab, because I couldn't walk, and when they went to take the blood it was incredibly thick. We went back home, Phil went back to work, and the phone rang soon after. It was Iowa City, and they said we needed to come right away, and that I needed to be admitted to the hospital, because I did have ovarian hyper-stimulation. I asked if I could wait for my husband to get home, and they said, "No. If you cannot find someone to bring you right now, we'll send an ambulance." There was danger of a blood clot or even kidney failure. My ovaries were severely swollen, and liquid was draining and depositing into my body… everywhere. After several days they were preparing to drain some of the fluid to decrease my extreme discomfort, but they found that my ovaries were so huge they couldn't do it without risking further injury.

It was one of the loneliest, most miserable times for me. I couldn't understand what God was doing. If I was pregnant, I would be in danger and would have to spend the next three months in the hospital. If I was not pregnant, I would start getting better within a week. I didn't even know what to hope for. I had worked so hard, and I wanted to have a baby, but I didn't want it to endanger my life.

After seven days, I noticed that the water was leaving my body, so I wasn't pregnant. When I went home, I just felt empty. I felt that God had made a promise to me but everything was falling apart. Phil was determined that we were not going through that again, but a few months later, I convinced him to give it another try. Since they knew how I reacted, they could monitor me more closely, and the process began again. This time it was uneventful, the embryos were implanted, and I felt really good.

We made the trip to Iowa City a few weeks later for the pregnancy test. Our whole family and many of our friends knew we were going that day, so we knew everybody was waiting on pins and needles at home (before the days when everyone had cell phones). I remember waiting for the nurse, and I had my head down just bracing for the worst, thinking, "I don't even want her to come back into this room and tell me it didn't work."

I heard her footsteps coming down the hall, and I just kept my eyes closed, and pretty soon she put her hands on the back of my shoulders and said, "Congratulations, it worked!"

I said, "Really?"

Then the phone rang at the doctor's office, and they said, "It's your sister."

At first I asked which one, but then I remembered that my sister Shelly had said, "I have to know right when you know, because I have my credit card ready, and I am going to go out and buy a ton of stuff," so I knew it was her.

I got on the phone and said, "Get out your credit card."

She started screaming, and we went home and told everyone. I was only two weeks pregnant, and the whole town knew.

My mom and I went to have my levels checked a few days later, and we were talking about cribs, and names, and whether or not it might be twins or triplets. When I got home, I went back to work. The phone rang, and the lady on the other side of the line said, "Mrs. Rich, I am really sorry, but your pregnancy is not viable. Your HGC levels didn't go up very much. Something's wrong. You're probably going to miscarry. Do you want a DNC?"

And I was just like, "Wait a minute."

I was so shocked I didn't even know what she was saying at first, and finally I was like, "No. I don't want a D&C. I want to give this baby a chance."

She responded with, "It's not really a baby. It's just cells."

I don't think I was very nice to her at that point. I told her that I believe in God and I believe in miracles. We continued to make the drive to Des Moines every couple of days, and it just confirmed what she was saying. The levels were going up just enough to make me continue to hope, but it wasn't really enough. I eventually did miscarry, and we had just one chance left.

We did some tests to discover why I had miscarried, because no one in my family ever had, so I thought it was weird. As it turned out, I have a rare blood disorder which causes my body to think an embryo is a foreign object, which in turn causes blood to clot around the embryo. So, for my last try, I had to give myself blood thinners each day. I was used to the shots, so no big deal.

I was really confident. I thought to myself, "Isn't this just like God? He waits until the very last try… This is the very last chance…" I just knew it was going to work, but when we went up for the pregnancy test, it was negative. Our last chance was gone. We were out of tries. We were definitely out of money. And we were also out of hope. I told God that my biological clock was ticking, just in case he didn't know.

We started to look into adoption, but we decided it was another uphill battle. We weren't ready for it, we had been through too much, and there had been too much disappointment. I couldn't take it again, and I finally said, "I give up."

I spoke these exact words to God: "You know what? If you really want me to have a baby, you're just going to have to drop one in my lap."

During this time I felt a closeness to God that I really hadn't had before. It is unexplainable. Most people would think, "What? Why? You're not getting what you think God should be giving you."

I did feel like I had a right to be angry, yet God was present with me. I did not understand what God was doing, but I decided to trust anyway. Then, on a Sunday afternoon, I was lying in a recliner, watching a lifetime movie after church, while Phil was on a hunting trip in Colorado. The phone rang, and it was the local doctor who had worked with us so tirelessly early on, and he started out by saying, "I don't quite know how to say this…"

There was immediate panic, because I had just had a pap two weeks earlier, and I thought to myself, "I have cancer."

But, finally, mercifully, this was not the bad news I was so used to at this point. Instead, he started over saying, "I don't quite know how to say this, but I just delivered a baby in the ER, and the mother says she is not leaving with the baby. I thought of you, and I think if you call a lawyer, you can take the baby home. She's beautiful, she's 6 pounds five ounces, she's perfect."

Was it a coincidence this doctor who had been with me from the very beginning was in the ER that day? I don't really think so. God doesn't control our actions and our coming and going, but there is certainly something to be said for the ways in which we can cooperate with God, listening to his promptings in our lives, and the people in my life had done this over and over again, bringing us to this moment.

But then I thought, "Oh. I have to call Phil!" And he had been saying that he really did not want to adopt! Again, no cell phone, so I had to call some relatives of some people he was with, and they reached him.

When he called me back, he said, "What's going on?" and when I told him, he said, "God was preparing me for that. I knew it had something to do with a baby. Go for it."

My response was, "*Who is this?*"

Well, our baby had to stay in the hospital for several days, as we took care of all the details, and during this time my mom and I went shopping for an outfit to bring her home in, and I had a meltdown right in the middle of the mall, because there I was shopping for a 'bringing the baby home outfit,' but I didn't have anything to bring the baby home *to*—no crib, no diapers, no bottles—I even started to worry that I might not have any motherly instincts! And then I thought, "What if my family doesn't accept this baby? What if my mom and dad don't think she's their 'real' grandkid?"

But the second any of us saw her, the second any of us held her, she was ours.

The day she came home, I was waiting at our house. I couldn't go get her, because we had to appoint a guardian, so we appointed the doctor who had delivered her to essentially 'deliver' her again. The whole family was there, looking out the window, when the red pick-up came down the road, and I just remember it so vividly. He got out of the truck and got this little car seat out, with a little pink blanket, and brought her up to us, and he was bawling, and so were we.

The first Sunday we brought her to church, the welcome was as if we were Princess Di and baby Harry! Phil pulled up with me, and there was a crowd… with cameras. We had our own paparazzi! There was hugging and crying, and when we sang, that day, I had never felt the words more sincerely.

Time went on, and we were so blessed to have Alexa, but there was also this nagging feeling. I felt bad for her, because I had such a good relationship with my brothers and sisters, and I wished she could have a sibling, but I knew that wasn't going to happen. I wished she could have a blood relative, because I thought that might be important to her someday, but I also knew that was not possible.

But two years later, the same mother and same father came to the same hospital, and the same doctor delivered PJ, who completed our family!

If anyone had tried to tell me, at the beginning of this journey, that it was going to take thirteen years and that I would actually be thankful (although, not for the miscarriage) that I was unable to bear biological kids, because I wouldn't have had the privilege of being the mother to *my* awesome kids, I never would have believed it!

I tell this story not because I want people to say, "Oh wow! What a great story," but because I want people to know that God will work in the lives of everyday people and even painful circumstances to do exceedingly more than we could imagine, as we partner with him on the journey.

Of course, this was only the beginning of the parenting journey for us. As of this writing, it's been almost twenty years since that red truck pulled up in our driveway. As a mom, I have always wanted the best for my children, but raising them has taught me some things about what it is to love and live into allowing the kind of freewill decisions that will shape their lives beyond my own control.

When my daughter graduated from high school, she really had no idea what she wanted to do with her life. She didn't want to go to college, which was difficult for me to deal with, but I finally accepted it and encouraged her to be open to listening for what God might have for her life. I always thought she exhibited the characteristics and qualities of a good nurse, but she was opposed to that, saying she did not want to have to bathe people.

As she continued to look for what she might want to do and be, she went on a mission trip to the Dominican Republic, and when she came back, she sat down and told us she felt called to go back as a missionary, working in the school for neglected children. She is working toward this now. Wouldn't it be something if a baby girl, given away at birth, goes on to love and help abandoned children? This is often too much for me to comprehend!

Ironically, I keep seeing *my* dreams fulfilled in her, as well, as she has to have a year of college before she can do her missions internship, so she is enrolled in classes now! In addition, the girl who wanted nothing to do with nursing saw an ad for nurses aids at our local Hospice Lodge and applied. She began working there; bathing people, changing their diapers, cleaning their dentures, and creating relationships with them; and she absolutely loves it! I often receive notes from families telling me how much they appreciate her and the witness she is for Jesus, to the dying. I never cease to be amazed. When she started the job, I told her to treat everyone like they are her grandparents. She kisses each one on the forehead when she leaves, she stayed late one night because a lady was afraid to go to sleep and just wanted her there, she read the Bible to a woman as she died. God is doing a wonderful work, and I am just sitting back, taking my hands off, and watching!

This brings me to the most incredible part yet. I was at work one day and got a call from an old classmate of mine whom I hadn't seen in years. He wanted to tell me his mother was at the Lodge, and he had met Alexa. He wanted to tell me how much he appreciated her care. Then he said, "This next part is awkward," and I braced myself thinking she had done something wrong.

He said, "My mother is Alexa's great-grandmother."

That really threw me! I didn't know any of the family, but I knew they were around. The last name was the last name of the biological father. He said his mother was the grandmother of the biological dad, and she had been very upset when both Alexa and PJ were given up. All these years I had no idea anyone in the family cared. Being a small town, she quickly found out where they were but never said anything or tried to see them. He said she was happy they were in a Christian home but sad she would never meet or know them. She had saved every newspaper clipping of the two of them over the years.

And then, when she was on her death bed, in walked Alexa, "like an angel." She instantly knew who she was but didn't say a word. He was not calling me so I would tell her, but he just wanted Phil and me to know.

We told her, and they had a happy reunion. Alexa took care of her for two more weeks before she died. She gave Alexa a ring that was given to her by her mother and gave PJ some arrowheads she found years ago.

And so, with a very great God and active participation of people listening to God's often quiet call, we have in a sense come full circle, and I have learned to get out of the way, not forcing my own plans and ideas, basking in blessings that have come in ways that were completely outside of what I thought I hoped for.

Kara Rich and her husband, Phil, have been married 31 years at the time of this writing. They reside in Chariton, Iowa, with their children, Alexa and PJ. Kara works as a receptionist at the local doctor's office and in her free time enjoys singing, photography, and spending time with her family.

Reconciling the God We Want to the God Who Is
L. Michaels

The Old Testament narrative of Job has intrigued me since I was a child. I was a weird kid. It's OK. Something I love most about Job is his lack of filters, because I can relate. Oh, how I can relate. But some stories are more difficult to tell than others.

Even in the midst of vomiting feelings and spilling my stuff all over the place, as a blogger, I went silent when faced with a health crisis, in part because it caused me to question whether or not the God we have was the god I wanted.

As a general rule, I am about as anti-drama as it gets. Granted, I love hyperbole, and I have been described as an excellent storyteller, so you have to understand that there are certainly aspects of dramatic flair, but the drama that causes blood pressure spikes and offense is just not for me. I thrive in high pressure, hard deadline, 11th hour moments, because I *like* the adrenaline rush. I have spent most of my life capable of being very cool in the midst of crisis (although I do cry afterward), but, as it turns out, I cannot function in *perpetual* crisis mode. I just can't. Really, who can?

Several years ago, my family was decorating our Christmas tree when I turned slightly to pick up my phone to take a picture of the kids. It was an incredibly normal thing to do. As I turned back, I heard a loud pop followed by multiple snapping noises. The noises were accompanied by a painful sensation traveling down my spine. I am stubborn and have a ridiculously high level of pain tolerance. I did not expect to find myself unable to crawl from my bed to the shower, without help, the next morning, and I was not nice to my husband when he forced me to go to redi-med. I was not nice, at all.

I was also not particularly nice when the redi-med doctor did not even look at my back and handed me three prescriptions. I think two were for pain and one was a muscle relaxant, and even though I did fill them, I threw them out, because reading about the potential side effects was more frightening than the pain.

I probably reached very, very, very not nice at some point during the several hours while I sat in the ER waiting room and then, when I was finally called back, a well meaning nurse followed the directions of *another* doctor who did not look at my back and shot something in my arm that allowed me to do incredible things such as floating around the room and walking on the ceiling. Seriously friends, I could never be a drug addict, because whether or not God and love are uncontrolling, *I* have some control issues, and I cannot be climbing walls!

Finally, a physical therapist came in and actually bothered to look at me. It took her less than four seconds to suck in a deep gasp and exclaim, "You popped your ribs!"

I had no idea what that meant. It sounded awful, but there was a certain sense of relief, because I do not like to feel as if I am crazy, and here was someone who was willing to validate the assumption that I am not. She spent about an hour trying to put my ribs back where they belonged, and she did, indeed, make some progress, but I left with a referral to see a spine doctor and more prescriptions in hand. I decided that I would take something for the pain. No, in retrospect, I don't think I actually decided that. I think I was still strung out on whatever they gave me at the ER and my husband probably force-fed me a Tylenol with Codeine, which is 100% guaranteed to knock me out within minutes. But the point is, I finally had some relief and some answers, with hope that more would come.

It took several weeks to get an appointment with the spine doctor. During this time, I did stupid things like traveling for hours on end and refusing pain meds unless I thought I was going to die. I think I popped two or three pills during this time. When I finally got in to see the spine guy, I explained that the PT at the ER said that I had popped my ribs, and he sort of chuckled, as if that was definitely not the issue. We talked for probably ten minutes or so, I described how I had injured myself taking a picture with my phone, and I am almost certain that we were heading down the, "Oh my goodness, why do they send me crazy patients," road, but he was very nice and finally decided to look at my back. He took a deep breath, exclaimed, "Oh!" and I knew I was probably not going to be committed any time soon.

He explained to me that he was adding a note to my chart stating that I was a very pleasant, reasonable, intelligent person. No kidding. I began to think that maybe, just maybe, this is the kind of injury that people do not normally endure while standing up and walking into doctors' offices on their own. He ordered an x-ray to determine whether or not I had also *broken* any ribs, and he ordered PT… for my ribs that were apparently no longer touching my spine where they should be.

I did the x-ray, and armed with a plan for how to resume normal life, Phil and I went out of our way to stop for dinner at The Cheesecake Factory, where I came pretty close to having a migraine, because I finally relaxed every muscle in my body for the first time in weeks. And for about an hour, life felt manageable again.

When we got back to the van, I realized that I had several missed calls and a voicemail. It was the phone number from the doctor's office. The only thing that came to mind was that I must, in fact, have broken ribs (well that stinks), so I called back to speak to the doctor whom I expected might actually not be at the office, because he had shared that he was going to see the new Star Wars Movie that night with his girlfriend and her kids, and, quite frankly, I thought it was probably well past time that he should have left to go home. Except, he hadn't left, because he was waiting for me to call back, because my chest x-ray showed a nodule on my left lung that required a CT scan.

Wait. Hold the phone. At this point, I know he's still talking and saying lots of affirming things like, "you're young, and you're otherwise healthy, and you don't smoke, and this is not an emergency, but I did send the order for the CT and you need to call on Monday to get it set up," and I'm entirely silent, and shaking, hearing it all but not processing any of it, really.

And I'm hating *this* adrenaline rush which would normally inspire fight or flight but has so overloaded my nervous system that I am completely frozen. I don't remember a whole lot more about that night, but I'm pretty sure it included things like trying to explain this phone conversation to my husband even though my mouth wasn't working and there were no words that made sense, and coming home to my computer where I spent far too many hours researching lung cancer while sitting next to my (then) five year old waiting for her to fall asleep after reading bedtime stories about cartoon animals.

Since non-emergency (yes, please try to define this for me) CT scans tend to be scheduled well in advance, I took the only quickly available option, 6:30 am on Christmas Eve morning, because this is, of course, what every mother of five wants to be prepping for on Christmas Eve, right? I made some decisions about who to share all of this with, and close friends with children who are close to my children didn't make the cut, because I could find no logical reason to risk scaring my kids half to death. I chose people whom I thought would pray hard and have no inclination to slip this information to my little people or tag me in a Facebook post that my teenagers might read. I did not share with extended family, either. It was easier for me that way. I did what I was capable of handling.

I have never felt so panicked and miserable on Christmas, but I hid it as well as I could. When the test results came back, every indicator, every... single... one... was sort of "middle of the road." The size of the nodule indicated that it may or may not be cancer. The shape of the nodule indicated that it may or may not be cancer. The composition of the nodule indicated that it may or may not be cancer. The location of the nodule indicated that it may or may not be cancer. The radiology report showed that *every* common non-cancerous cause had been eliminated, but that because there were no high risk factors in my life (minus family history), they still believed the nodule to *likely* be benign. I am a detail person. I need to know things with some amount of certainty. I don't necessarily need to know *everything*, although that *is* helpful, but I need to know *something*. I just couldn't deal with any of that.

The suggested option was to wait and to do another CT scan in eight weeks to see if the nodule was growing. The only other real option was a needle biopsy that would require puncturing the chest wall and possibly leading to a collapsed lung because of the location of the nodule. I have never been such a mess in a doctor's office. Waiting eight weeks seemed stupid. Subjecting my body to testing that could do much more harm than good seemed (at least) equally stupid. And there was *seriously* no indicator that might sway me one direction or the other? None? I asked my doctor (late twenties or early thirties with two babies at home) what she would do if it was her. She said she would wait the eight weeks and do the next CT scan. With much anxiety, I decided to go ahead and follow that suggestion. I hadn't slept in days. There was no way I could make a calculated decision on my own.

I spent the next eight weeks doing things that are outside the norm for me, some of them by far. In my desperation to get some sleep, with all of the typical things I might try (essential oils and lavender candles and running myself into the ground and stuff) failing miserably, I went through the rest of the Tylenol with Codeine. I tried herbal teas. I read and read and read until my eyes should have slammed shut. I watched more TV than I had in my entire adult life. I drank a beer for the first time ever. I listened to music. I put blankets up over my windows. Sleep did not come in more than a couple of hours at a time, here and there, for the most part. There were a few times when my body was exhausted enough to shut down in the middle of the day. All of the natural rhythms ceased to exist.

I booked flights to conferences and weekends away with friends. I hated flying, but since I was relatively convinced I was dying, anyway, I figured it was worth the risk. What's a couple of months in the grand scheme of things? If a plane crashed, it crashed. But there was more to it than this.

I started pulling *way* back from my husband and kids. I wrote a letter to my husband about all the stuff he should do if I died first, and I posted it to my personal blog and stood back and watched how he would react, how my oldest kids would react, how everyone in the world (or at least everyone in *my* world) would react. After that, I was not convinced that he thought he could do it... life... without me. It absolutely killed me to be sitting at the airport in Las Vegas while my daughter melted down at a quiz meet, halfway across the country, and my well meaning friends with no knowledge of this crisis, surrounded her saying things like, "It's hard when Mom's not here, isn't it," and one of my sweet friends who *did* know what was going on surrounded me by sending me live updates on how the finals round was going.

But I had to know that my family had people. I'm a stinking hover mom! I stopped hovering, because I was acutely aware that I might not be able to keep doing it. I needed to see the kids depending on Phil. I needed to see that people would come around them and love them if I couldn't. We have really good people, but it made me want to throw up.

I pulled back *at* home, too. I needed to know that the laundry and dishes would get done whether I was there or not and that somebody would read to "the baby" and that at the very least everybody could cook something hot for themselves, even if it was just toast. Ideally, parents are supposed to work themselves out of a job at some point, but this was an accelerated process.

Over the course of the next eight weeks, I took a philosophy class at Northwest Nazarene University, and there is a certain amount of irony to the timing and the subject matter. I had taken a class with Tom Oord during a previous term, in what seemed like a different lifetime, and the truth is I had hated his ideas and the ways in which they challenged me to reconsider my views of God and love. In the ensuing years, I had mellowed and grown, and I was extremely excited about the upcoming class… until I was in crisis! Even though I didn't legitimately want to, I continued to push back against the idea of a God who cannot do *everything*, because it scared me that we might have a god who cannot do *anything* and especially that God might not do *the thing* I needed God to do! I recognized some tendencies about myself, including the fact that I really need a god who is in control when I feel out of control. I don't think that's the god we get, but it can be very tempting to return to that kind of thinking and praying when our circumstances are urgent.

Tom (who knew nothing of my health dilemma and quite possibly wondered why I was such a jerk) responded to my vague concerns by reminding me that if God is open and persistently, lovingly working for our good, then our stories are not yet written and unchangeable. This is precisely why our communication with God, our prayers, and our participation matter.

You might think (or at least hope) that grasping such personal and intimate relationship with God would be enough to neatly wrap up this story, but we live in the real world. It sometimes seems as if there is never enough space for lament, and even though I wish we didn't, we need that space.

When the eight weeks had passed and the second CT scan approached, I hit the wall hard at full force. For most of my life, I have been prone to worry but not prone to full-fledged anxiety or panic attacks. I might be concerned, but I have it under control. The day before the scan, rocking back and forth on the bathroom floor and just about pulling my hair out, I had to tell Phil to take the kids to his mom's for the night, because I just couldn't handle being in the same space as them and having them find me like this. He packed them up quickly and got them out of the house.

Scan #2 came back exactly the same as the first one. This was really great news and allowed me to relax a little bit for a little while. There was still the fact that every indicator told us absolutely nothing, but the nodule had not grown. It had not grown at all. Cancer supposedly grows at a certain rate, so there was some relief. Because I had done so much research at this point, there wasn't as much relief for me as there would have been for someone typical who would just take the results for what they were, but some relief was better than no relief. We scheduled a third scan, six months out. I slept a little better over the next few months. We told our oldest two kids about what had been going on, because they're really smart, and they deserved to know why I was a little crazy... and absent... and not myself, as of late. Their reactions were different from one another and both equally difficult to process. Essentially, my oldest son let go so much it hurt, and my oldest daughter held on so tight it hurt. It all just hurt.

After some amount of time, I began to panic that we were waiting too long, that we were going to do the third scan and find that the nodule was, indeed, growing and that we missed it because we did the second scan too early and the third one too late. I started playing with numbers in my head, and, let's face it, that's just a terrible plan for a non-numbers person. The build up to the upcoming CT got more and more difficult, because I didn't really feel like I had anyone to debrief with. I was sick of scaring my family. I have great friends, but all of them (who were aware) seemed pretty confident that I was OK, based on the second scan. I couldn't continue to talk about it, because I didn't have anything new to say, and I didn't want people to get tired of talking to me. I didn't want to make something out of nothing, but I needed some people to talk to, even if I was just repeating the same thing over and over again. I chose silence, though, even though it didn't feel good. Ordinarily, I am a listener. I am a problem solver. I feel most alive when I am helping other people. And yet I was so wrapped up in my own disaster, I found myself with nothing left to give *and* nothing left to say.

I pulled myself together, enough, before the third scan that I did not have to drop my kids off with Grandma. I did another early morning CT, and I went straight home and proceeded to take a six hour nap. I know you can't really call that a nap. Whatever. I decided not to contact my doctor's office. I decided not to make an appointment for test results. I decided that I would know what I needed to know when I needed to know it and that if nobody called me quickly, there was probably nothing too pressing, too catastrophic, too deadly. I got an email a couple of days later telling me that there had, again, been absolutely no change. Because the nodule had been this consistent for eight months, my doctor was relatively confident that it is scar tissue of some sort.

We scheduled one last scan for another 15 months out. I spent most of that time feeling OK, and I even decided to maintain some of my new life rhythms (flying and conferencing and soul care), because I liked them. Regardless of previous test results, I still spent too much time either convinced that I was dying of lung cancer or at least concerned that I might be. But, here's the thing. I'm not. *I'm not.* I am not dying any faster than anyone else. After two years of anxiety and panic attacks, sprinkled with CT scan radiation and a little bit of insanity; what I would have liked was a definitive note that read, "This is definitely not cancer, it never has been, it never will be, thanks for playing along, as a parting gift you will never, ever die."

But, here's what I got instead: "Left lower lobe nodule has demonstrated stability for 24 months and is likely a benign abnormality."

Close enough. I can live with that. Literally. Hopefully for a very long time. But, the reality is, my healthy lungs and I could be hit by a bolt of lightning, tomorrow. We all know that life is short. It's always shorter than we hoped it would be. Always. But we can't stop living.

This journey caused me to think more about suffering, prayer, and presence and how it all comes together, but I don't think it was necessary. What I mean by this is that I don't think God wanted this to happen, nor do I think God needed this to happen in order to bring about some greater good. What I do think is that God can use everything—even crap like this—and God has done so, as I have listened to God's persuasive voice in my life, even when I couldn't listen to much of anything at all.

I am not glad that I went through this! I am glad that I am a different person than I was at the onset. I think there might have been better ways to get there, but whatever… I'm there. I am braver. I am willing to take more risks. I am less concerned about what other people think of me and more concerned about other people, in general. And I know I have not yet "arrived." I fully recognize that if I have a goal or a dream, I had better start chasing it right now, because even if I have inherited the genetic make-up of the women on my dad's side of the family, a hundred years will never be enough—not for me, not for you, not for anyone. So, breathe in, breathe out, and repeat ad nauseam even if it makes you sick, because it totally beats the alternative.

L Michaels is a follower of Jesus; Ph.D. student in Liturgical Studies at Boston University; author of numerous commentaries, articles, book chapters, and blog posts; editor; wife; mom; and aspiring peacemaker. She has an M.A. and M.Div. (both in theology/spiritual formation) from Northwest Nazarene University. L writes and podcasts about theology, the sacraments, and ministry to the least of these at Flip Flops, Glitter, and Theology (.com). In her spare time, L likes to sit by the ocean and drink voluminous amounts of Peppermint Bark Mocha.

flipflopsglitterandtheology.com

What's Wrong and What's Right
Henry Sweeney

I was an active High School student. Being from a small Christian School, I played every sport that was offered. When I was not playing sports at school, I was heavily involved at church. There was always something that kept me going but when you hear the words, "I don't know what's wrong with you," it really makes an impact on your life.

These are words that a 16 year old should never have to hear. Modern medicine has come so far since those words were spoken to me in the fall of 1996. I could not have imagined the journey I would travel over the next 20+ years of my life...

I remember the season clearly. My family and I had taken a trip to Indiana to visit some friends for Thanksgiving—a trip we had taken several times and friends we had known for years. This year would be different. We arrived on a Tuesday after an uneventful drive. Wednesday began with what I thought was a stomach virus. After several hours of pain followed by brief moments of relief, I realized that it was more. I didn't want to eat. Food was placed in front of me, and I simply could not stomach the sight. Thursday, Friday, and Saturday passed, and the story remained the same. I noticed my clothes were getting a little baggy. The drive home, on Sunday, was long and painful. Monday morning, I was back in school seemingly doing better and passing it off as a simple fluke, but by mid-week I could not stand up. Every move I made caused severe pain. My parents took me to my pediatrician who sent me to the hospital after several in-office tests. I arrived at Children's National Medical Center in Washington D.C., and after more hours of testing, the doctor walked into the room and said, "I don't know what's wrong with you".

The only thing I knew was that I had lost 51 pounds in less than a week—51 pounds! I was finally released from the hospital with no answers and a lot of medication that *might* help my symptoms. A week later, I was back in the hospital.

This visit was a little different. I was greeted by a different doctor, Dr. John S. Latimer. He was the leading Gastroenterologist for pediatrics in the Mid-Atlantic region. I felt a little more confident in his abilities. After just one simple test and a few hours looking over my previous tests, he came into my room with a diagnosis. That diagnosis was Crohn's Disease. It is an intestinal disorder that causes severe inflammation and closure of the bowel. The only remedy for Crohn's at the time was extensive in-patient treatment with heavy medication with severe side effects. It was the worst four weeks I ever spent in the hospital (or maybe anywhere).

Over the next twenty years, I bounced from medication to medication. Some medications worked well, and others only caused more pain. There was no prognosis for a permanent, or even long-term, solution. The only thing that was certain was uncertainty. Trial and error was the only way to handle this disease. Among the side effects was extreme weight fluctuation that spanned 100 pounds. Doctor after doctor and medication after medication caused pain, with no hope of relief.

I graduated from high school a year after my diagnosis. It was not an easy task. There were many days missed due to illness and visits to doctors. In the fall, I entered my freshmen year at Trevecca Nazarene University. I was following the call of the Lord on my life to pursue full time ministry. While at Trevecca, I met my amazing wife, Amber. We were married in February 2002, and she has been a constant source of support and love over these past fifteen years. During our marriage we have seen the ups and downs of my physical condition, but she has been by my side since the day we met. We have two wonderful children, Elizabeth (13 at the time of this writing) and William (10). My physical struggles have affected my entire family and become part of our story.

In the midst of the physical battles and struggles, God was calling our family to leave all we knew as stable. In 2015, God asked us to leave our jobs, sell our house, and move away from Maryland. I finished out that school year at Grace Brethren Christian School, and we resigned our positions at Melwood Church of the Nazarene, in June. We put our house on the market and received two offers on the first day, one which was over our asking price! Our real estate agent, a close family friend, said that she had not seen a home in our market sell that fast in a long time. There was a high inventory of properties and a low demand, yet our property sold in less than 24 hours! Change can be difficult, but little did we know that this would be the best thing that could have happened for my health.

On the day we planned to move, I found myself in the hospital in Maryland. Our house had been sold, our truck had been packed, and we were ready to leave, but the doctor who came into the ER said we had to head to surgery, instead. There was a large abscess in my left side. The abscess was from a rupture in my large intestine. The reality and severity of my condition had become a realization. All the conversations that doctors had over the years about probabilities of surgery were coming true. I had made it over two decades without surgery, but now I was faced with my biggest fear. A three hour surgery to remove the abscess was the beginning of a long chapter in my life.

Three weeks after surgery, I was able to safely join my wife and kids in Georgia. Upon my arrival, I connected with a great team of doctors. They immediately ordered some tests and lab work to be done. After a few short days, I was called back into the doctors' office for a consultation. The conversation was brief, and honestly I don't remember a lot about that day other than the words, "You need to see the surgeon."

What's Wrong and What's Right

I knew that it was coming.

In October, I visited Atlanta Colorectal Surgeons—the scariest visit I have had since my diagnosis. Dr. Evan Feldman, a young doctor maybe in his mid 30's, sat me down and drew a picture of what was going on. He said these words, "We need to remove the nasty parts."

I questioned what that would mean and when it had to happen, and he said, "Soon."

Within weeks, I went back for a visit with Dr. Feldman. I walked in under my own power but would not walk out of his office that way. I entered the room and when they took my vitals, my heart rate was 165 beats per minute—twice the normal rate. Immediately he sat me down and called my wife, telling her that I was being taken straight to the Emergency Room. He did not even want me to walk on my own. The next few hours were a blur, but I think they put me through some tests and lab work. At the end of it all, I was told I had sepsis—an infection that had entered my blood stream. After a night on intravenous medications, I was beginning to show signs of improvement. The next day I was told that I would need to, "give my bowels a rest," which meant I would be fed through an IV for the foreseeable future. Life was miserable. Then Dr. Feldman came into my room and said he had a possible solution that would allow me to eat. He said he could give me a temporary Ileostomy. A small section of my small intestine would be pulled through my stomach wall and drained into a bag. It sounded pretty gross, and it was at first, but at least it would give me the ability to eat. We decided to go ahead with the procedure. Two hours of surgery later, and I had a new 'friend' sticking out of my stomach wall. My family named it Frank. I was now the proud owner of an Ostomy. That's not how I would have expected to spend my life, but the surgery changed me for the better.

However, in March, I was back in the hospital. Same story. Tests, lab work, and more diagnoses. I needed more extensive surgery sooner rather than later. We scheduled this surgery for April 18, 2016 at 12:00 pm. The anticipation of that day was draining. It was as if time simply slowed down. Days seemed to drag on and on. We arrived at the hospital around 9:00am only to find that I was actually scheduled for surgery an hour earlier than expected. There was no more time to sit and wait or think, just a quick walk back to get everything started. Six to Seven hours of surgery, which only seemed like five minutes to me, and I was done. My entire large intestine was removed. I still had my Ostomy, but twenty plus years of dealing with Crohn's at its worst was over, and I was going to live better than ever. After pain medication and a good night's sleep, Dr. Feldman came in to see me the next day. He said words that will affect the rest of my life: "I have been doing this surgery for years and I have never seen a large intestine as swollen or infected as yours."

My life would look much different from that day until now.

I wish that was where the story of my physical struggles ended, but it is not. To celebrate this new chapter in my life, my family decided to take a cross country road trip. In June, we hooked up the travel trailer and headed to California. We made stops at some of the most beautiful

What's Wrong and What's Right

portions of the Southern United States. We saw landmarks and experienced some of God's amazing creation. On our way back, we stopped for a bit in Barstow, California. I had a severe headache and some other things were just not right. I talked myself, and my wife, into taking me to the local community hospital. Blood tests were run and after about 3 hours of waiting the doctor came in and said, "Dude, I have had dead people come into this place with higher blood counts than you. How are you even standing and talking to me?"

My hemoglobin level was 3.8 as opposed to the normal 11. After a trip to the ICU, and seven units of blood, I was released to the care of my family. We made our way home and eventually arrived back in Georgia. The cycle of doctor's visits resumed, and I was put on medication for my blood level issues. I heard everything from low iron to blood clots in my spleen, and there were still no answers for what was going on in my body. My levels finally stabilized, but months later I was met again with the words, "I don't know how you are functioning."

Would this never end?

There have been many times in my life when the words of a very popular hymn by Horatio Spafford have run through my mind. The words of that first verse define so much of my story:

When peace like a river, attendeth my way,
When sorrows like sea billows roll,
Whatever my lot, thou hast taught me to say,

Henry Sweeney

It is well, it is well, with my soul.[1]

Throughout my journey, I have struggled to say the words, "It is well with my soul." As a person in ministry, I have walked difficult roads with other people. I have seen families through the loss of loved ones, illness, broken relationships and other dark moments in their lives. This was different for me. I have never been the one to need others to help me through hard times and especially to remind me of the nearness of God. I had preached sermons, taught lessons, and read books about how to rely on God when you most need Him, but through these hard times, I had to put those things into practice in my own life. Until I was 16, I never knew what that meant. I would learn, and I still am learning. I learned what it means to lean into God. I have never felt as if God left me or as if God did not care, but at times I had to remind myself to rely on God more than my circumstances. When medications would not work, when doctors didn't have answers, when my faith was tested by those who didn't believe; I had to lean on God's unfailing love for me. I knew God was there, working in my life, but the tangible expressions became vitally important. I saw, for the first time, what people meant when they said they just needed to feel God drawing near. If it had not been for God using people— doctors, family, our church families across state lines, and others in my life; I am sure the journey would not have

---

[1] American Colony, and Horatio Gates Spafford. *Draft manuscript copy of hymn "It is Well With My Soul" by Horatio Gates Spafford.* to 1878, 1873. Manuscript/Mixed Material. Retrieved from the Library of Congress, <https://www.loc.gov/item/mamcol.016/>.

been tolerable.

It has amazed me, during this physical journey, how God has been there at every point, guiding me through every surgery and present in each hospital room. God never left me... not even once... and God will never leave me no matter what I am going through. I have seen Him working through the lives of doctors and nurses. I have seen His compassion in the eyes of hospital workers that brought me dinner and cleaned my room, encouraging and helping me, even when that was not their job. In every moment, God used willing people to be instruments of grace in my life.

This brings with it fresh perspective on how God works in the lives of people that are suffering. At times along this journey, I have needed God to be close in different ways. Sometimes I needed God to remind me of his constant presence to get me through the many valleys in my story. There were numerous times I needed God to be my provider. Throughout my physical struggles, as you might be able to guess, I could not hold down a full time job. Actually, I could not even hold down a part time job! I never knew when I was going to have to enter the hospital again, so there was little reason hope when seeking employment. It is amazing to look back and see how God provided for our family during those times. I think back to the sale of our home in Maryland. When we set the price of our home, we were not thinking of long-term financial stability. We simply thought it would be good for us to have the equity as a nest egg for the next step in our lives. Well, the amount that we profited from the sale of our house has been exactly enough to provide for our needs since we left Maryland. It has been a comfort to know that God has met our needs.

I have mentioned, in my struggles, that there have been many people who have been expressions of God's love and grace in my life. There has been a steady flow of people whom God has prompted to be exactly where I needed them at any given time. I think about the Jewish doctor, Dr. John S. Latimer, who first diagnosed me, the amount of knowledge that he shared about Crohn's Disease, and his willingness to try and help as often as he could. He was continually thinking about what was the best option for my health and longevity. He would call my parents with the newest possibilities, and when he would enter a new area of treatment, he would always ask if I was willing to try it if he thought I would be a good candidate. I saw the frustration in his eyes when something would not work. When I suffered severe headaches, he took that home to his wife, who was a neurologist, and discussed it at dinner. Most doctors I have encountered in my life only saw me as a number as opposed to a real person, but Dr. Latimer was different. To him, I was not a statistic or a way to earn a few extra dollars. I truly felt as if I was his only patient and that no matter what, he was going to do everything he could to help me, even if that meant keeping me as a patient well beyond my pediatric years. He truly served as the hands and feet of God to me.

I hated changing doctors, including moving from one state to another. Often, when you change doctors, they feel the need to start over. It made for a crazy few months, beginning with the search process.

What's Wrong and What's Right

How in the world does a person go about finding new doctors in a new place? How would I know who was best—whom I could trust? A simple search of providers who were covered by my insurance, and a weird connection from the surgeon in Maryland that knew a gastroenterologist in Georgia, led me to a great group of doctors located twenty minutes from our new location in Georgia. My first visit to this office was extremely unusual. I entered that office thinking that it was awkward. I was visiting a doctor whom I had never known or even seen before, one who was younger than I was. How could this person help me? Once I entered that exam room and the discussions began, God put all my fears to rest. Dr. Nadia Stanford and her team of nurses handled my needs far better than I could have hoped. They saw the fear and anxiety in my eyes and did everything they could to put me at ease. I have had several bad experiences with doctors in my many years, and this one was different. There was a fresh new feeling that came over that room. They knew what they were talking about. These new individuals were exactly who I needed—the team who ended up saving my life. They knew when to say when and that the only treatment was to have a surgeon get involved in the picture. They were allowing themselves to be used as instruments of God's grace.

Although I have had the opportunity to share pieces of my story from various platforms, there is a portion of my story that I have not shared yet. My wife Amber and I had been on staff at Melwood Church of the Nazarene since 2001. Fifteen years of ministry is amazing. Fifteen years of ministry in one geographic location is almost unheard of!

Melwood was my home church. From days after my birth through all those years of ministry, it was a place of stability. At Melwood there is a saying, "You may leave the congregation, but you never leave the Melwood family," and that is very true.

There was a sense there that you were more than a body occupying a pew, but that you were a person who had needs, and the church body did everything it could to meet your needs. During the first few years of my diagnosis the church drew close to me and my family. I can still remember when I was in the hospital, and the church softball team got together and signed a softball for me to have as a reminder of their love for me. Every person in that church was a part of the lives of everyone else, in a good way. We cried together. We laughed together. We did life together.

When we relocated to Georgia, we found ourselves in a very unusual position, searching for a new church. Of course, being in the midst of the ongoing physical battles in my life, we needed a church family that was going to be a place of strength in our life as a family, and I especially needed it to be a place that was extremely supportive of Amber and the kids. The 'local' Nazarene church was almost forty-five minutes from our home and was not a good fit for us. We looked for sister denominations in the area but did not feel at home in any of those settings. In November, we decided that we were going to try one last church before we settled. We had passed this church a number of times in our daily travels to doctors and hospitals but really never noticed. Amber did some research, and their beliefs were close to ours, so we decided to attend one Sunday. We were met at the door by two gentlemen, Jimmy and Jim. We shook hands; and the next thing I knew, I felt at home. We entered the foyer of Bethany Christian Church, and a peace came over us that could not be explained. We sat through the service and got a great visitors' gift, a coffee mug. Any church that freely offers coffee mugs already has a leg up on any other church! We meet the senior minister and a few other people from the congregation. There was no pressure from them to make sure we got plugged in or took on a new ministry. They just wanted to love on our family. We had no idea how much that day would change our story. A few weeks later, we returned to Bethany and spent fifteen minutes after service meeting new people who would later turn out to be part of our story in a different way. Our family had truly found a new church family. We experienced, and are experiencing, the love of God through His people in a new way. In early 2016, we decided to begin involving ourselves in the ministry of the church. I was willing to begin serving on the audio visual crew and Amber was singing and began as Children's Minister. We started attending a Sunday School class. This class is a mix of generations, and each one has a different story of God's amazing grace in their lives. That class is taught by Tommy Musick, a great teacher with a great teaching style. His wife Tena attends that class as well. A few months in, Tena approached Amber and me about starting a small group. God had just provided a new home for them, and they wanted to begin hosting a small group but did not want to lead the Bible study portion. We took a few weeks and answered yes to that opportunity. Two weeks later we had our first meeting at their home, with eight people, and I am excited to report that at our last meeting we had forty-three! I know that is more like a small church, but it is exactly what we all need. We started this small group shortly after my surgery in April 2016. We have prayed through lack of employment, sickness, job transitions, job frustrations, loss of loved ones, including my father in April of 2017, and family needs. We have done life together. We have spent hours laughing together, studying together, and crying together. We have seen God move in ways that none of us could have ever expected. This group has impacted my family in amazing ways. When I was in California and suffering illness many miles from home, they called, sent text messages, and simply showed God's love from across the country. We have kept eyes and ears open for job possibilities and ways that we could meet each other's needs. There is also a major tangible way that this group has been at work in our lives. In August of 2017, Amber received a text message from Tena asking if Amber would be interested in a position as an After School Director. Amber did not feel as if that was a position she wanted to fill, so Tena asked if I would be interested. I interviewed for that position and was offered the job on the spot. It has been such a place of ministry, all because God's people were doing exactly what they are supposed to do: supporting one another. I cannot begin to express how much this group has meant to our family. They have truly *become* our family.

I could go on and on naming people and describing stories of how God has worked in my life through those people, but I want to close my story by expressing how amazing it is to see God's people at work.

What's Wrong and What's Right

Throughout my life, I have seen the need for people. When I ministered, I saw God in the lives of people. I saw God working with humanity in ways that only God could work. I cried with people who had been delivered and whose needs had been met. I expressed how God could work in their lives and what it meant to work with God. I spoke the truth that He would use people to offer healing, peace, provision and comfort in their lives. I shared Scripture and truths about God's never failing love for His people. All of that was and is true. Somehow, though, when it came to me as an individual, I struggled from time to time. I knew God was present, and I knew the power of His truth in my life. I knew that desperate need for people to be used by God, but it was hard to accept it. Were there days when I wondered about the presence of God in the midst of everything? Sure. I would not be human if I did not wonder or wrestle with the presence of God. I am here today as one who has had to deal with the question, "How do you lean into God and cooperate with him?"

I stand as one who, along this journey, has seen the need for God's people to be exactly what I needed to show mercy, grace, and love in my life and in the life of my family. I have searched and sought answers, but the words that I heard twenty years ago, "I don't know what's wrong with you," still linger in my head.

I have walked this path of pain and suffering and had it not been for the community of God being at work in my life, this path would be unbearable.

My journey, our journey as a family, is not over and we look forward to seeing how God will work in our lives. We are certain of one thing and that is that God's people have played, and will play, a huge role in our story. I am reminded of the words of Paul to the church at Philippi:

> *So if there is any encouragement in Christ, any comfort from love, any participation in the Spirit, any affection and sympathy, complete my joy by being of the same mind, having the same love, being in full accord and of one mind. Do nothing from selfish ambition or conceit, but in humility count others more significant than yourselves. Let each of you look not only to his own interests, but also to the interests of others. Have this mind among yourselves, which is yours in Christ Jesus, who, though he was in the form of God, did not count equality with God a thing to be grasped...*[2]

This is the story of God's people. That we look not only to ourselves but, maybe more importantly, we look out for each other—we seek ways in which we can be the expression of God to those around us. We need to be mindful of those who do not, or cannot, experience God apart from His people. We are called to be the body that builds up and edifies each other, so we can show His love to the world. I believe that when the people of God allow themselves to be used as instruments of grace, they are truly fulfilling the call of God on their lives. We are not placed on this earth, on this journey, to go through it by ourselves. May we listen to God as he calls us to the place where he wants us to be in life,

---

[2] Phil 2:1-7

so that we can interact with creation.

Henry Sweeney grew up in a small community outside of Washington D.C.
He graduated from Grace Brethren Christian School in 1996.
Henry continued his education at Trevecca Nazarene University and graduate with a Bachelor of Arts degree in religion in 2001. He later went on to receive his Master of Arts in Spiritual Formation from Northwest Nazarene University in 2014.
He served as an Associate Pastor to Youth in Maryland until 2015.
He married his wife, Amber, in 2002, and they have 2 wonderful children.
Henry and Amber now serve at a church in West Georgia.

"The Lord Be With You"
Part One: A Philosophy of Presence
Tim Reddish

Strange as it may sound, I think many Western Christians today are no longer willing to genuinely *believe* in the Jesus-story—assuming they did earlier. Some have simply lost *confidence* in the gospel. The problem is not simply a matter of whether or not one accepts as historical fact that Jesus of Nazareth actually lived; there is little doubt that he did. Nor is it really a question of the veracity of Jesus' teaching, or the church's views on the significance of his deeds, death, and resurrection. Rather, it concerns the *relevance* of those matters for today. "Relevance" has a purely utilitarian tone; what *practical* difference does it make? As an academic who values knowledge and wisdom for their own sake, I find this a sad reflection on our times. Perhaps this is only to be expected in a *technological* age. After all, most of us are only concerned with the functionality of our laptops and phones, and have no real interest in the software and hardware—let alone the underlying principles of semiconductor physics. The issue of relevance is a fixed feature of our consumer world, and this frustrates practitioners of education as well as pastors. Add to that the sense of entitlement and immediacy—wanting it all and wanting it now—means that the notions of patience and discipline are inevitably going to be unpopular in our fast-paced, throw-away society.

This matter of relevance ("Why do we *need* God?") is also closely connected to the comfortable lifestyles of the Western middle classes. Most of us have some sort of social safety net (healthcare, benefits, pensions, savings, and insurances of various kinds) that was unheard of in previous centuries, let alone in biblical times. And anesthetics and painkillers protect us from the harsh reality of suffering, at least to a degree. It is only when our routines are invaded by uncertainty and insecurity, to the point that we are no longer feel 'in control' of our personal choices and destiny, that the relevance question is revisited. Religious faith is, for some, the last insurance policy—a desperate hope when all else fails. But grasping for relevance in a crisis is hardly ideal, not to mention somewhat hypocritical! Even so, I believe *how* the Christian faith addresses the troubling problem of suffering *does* provide a valid response to the question of relevance.[1] But this reply is not a simplistic cure-all, or a definitive "answer," or even "proof" of Christianity. For, as dedicated followers of Jesus know from personal experience, faith seeks understanding even in the complex issue of evil and suffering. And that faith provides a firm hope for the journey, one that—when all is said and done along the way—ultimately trusts in resurrection beyond death. That being the case, perhaps it is not surprising most seek hedonistic alternatives for the here and now!

Nevertheless, however comfortable our lifestyles, we all die eventually. It is fair to say that *death* remains *the* taboo subject of Western culture. We even avoid using that word. Death comes too soon or too late for most people. If we are honest, we do not even want to face the issue of our own mortality. And, naturally, the fear of the process of dying lies—often hidden, but still present—in the darkest recesses of our minds. Having said that, the reality of suffering and death provides us with the opportunity to address the basic question of the relevance of life itself.

So, *are* our lives parts of a bigger story, one that might involve life after death? Instead of exploring that possibility, many quickly shut down the enquiry. If there *is* a bigger story it might have implications for our sense of freedom—and that is troubling for some. A prior belief in our personal autonomy and moral independence would be brought into question if there were an overarching metanarrative to history. This, then, is a key feature in the matter of relevance. If there *is* a bigger story, we

---

[1] See Oord, *The Uncontrolling Love of God: An Open and Relational Account of Providence*, InterVarsity (2015); Reddish, *Does God Always Get What God Wants?*, Cascade (2018).

would be forced to acknowledge there is something Lesslie Newbigin calls "public truth."[2] In this context it is that the Christian view of history, from creation to the eschaton (and beyond), has universal intent. In other words, it is a narrative that is true or valid for everyone. This narrative should not be understood purely in terms of a sequence of historical incidents, but includes the meaning or significance of those events. For those who believe in God, this means incorporating a *theological* layer of understanding to history. Consequently, while a scientific account of origins (big bang, evolution, chance and necessity)[3] provides a materialistic description of creation, it must be incorporated into a broader theology of nature.[4]

Of equal importance, however, is the question of history's ultimate destiny. Astronomers tell us that in a few billion years, the sun will become a "red giant" and expand to engulf our planet. This will occur once all the sun's hydrogen has been converted to helium through nuclear fusion. However, life on Earth will become unviable long before then, because the sun will become hot enough to boil our oceans in about a billion years' time! In light of that fate, one can perhaps see why there is a fascination with science fiction; interstellar travel is our only salvation—should pollution, war, or a giant meteor not finish us off first! We have evolved to a point where we recognize that humankind, as individuals and as a species, is finite.

---

[2] See Newbigin, *Truth to Tell: The Gospel as Public Truth,* Eerdmans (1991).
[3] See Reddish, *Science and Christianity: Foundations and Frameworks for Moving Forward in Faith,* Wipf & Stock (2016).
[4] A great deal of thought and debate has already been given to that task.

The Christian brings a crucial dimension to that bleak outlook, however ingenious and creative we may become, namely God and God's engagement with history. The study of 'end matters'—eschatology—is, of necessity, a matter of faith. But it is not a privatized faith; it has universal intent and hence is public truth, even if we do not really know all the details of what the eschaton entails. Sadly, some churches spend far too much time speculating on what is, for the most part, unknowable and seem to promote their views with absolute certainty. Some of those eschatological pronouncements are akin to conspiracy theories; I suggest you ignore them! Nevertheless, it would be a serious miscalculation to dismiss the matter altogether. Clearly a person's view of end matters informs their response to the question of relevance. If you don't believe in life after death, or in a linear storyline to history, it is not that you believe in nothing. It means you are already committed—consciously or subconsciously—to a different narrative.

There is another important feature of relevance and eschatology, namely a deep desire for ultimate *justice*.[5] It is obvious that we all want justice for *ourselves*! A crucial theme within Christianity, however, is that in the end God will bring about justice *for all*. What that 'heaven' will actually look like is beyond our imagination, but that should not cause us to belittle that vision. Too often we imagine an afterlife that is serene and beautiful. But that is surely not enough, especially for those whose life experience has been one of a downtrodden and disadvantaged people.

---

[5] Rutledge, *The Crucifixion: Understanding the Death of Jesus Christ,* Eerdmans (2015), 128-132.

Heaven must (at least) entail peace *with justice*; the latter cannot be left undone.

A feature of the Old Testament prophets was their cry for social justice;[6] they spoke "truth to power"—often at a dire personal cost. Jesus followed in that mold. Christians believe that "God's righteous activity is setting to right what is wrong."[7] Given the current state of the world, we may have serious doubts about that claim! Nevertheless, that is a fixed feature of the Christian hope, founded on the life, death, and resurrection of Jesus—where the Trinitarian God decisively dealt with evil, personally. The resurrection demonstrates that evil will *not* have the last word. It is God's emphatic NO to evil and injustice, and YES to life. Consequently, those who downplay the reality of the resurrection diminish the Christian hope that evil will ultimately be overcome. There is much more to the cross' theological significance, of course, but it is foundational to the issue of relevance of ultimate justice for all.

I have stated that I think part of the mainline church's present problems is that it has lost confidence in the overall Christian narrative, and especially of its eschatology. Some, understandably, ignore end time matters altogether out of fear of being tainted by fanciful forms of eschatology (and thereby ruining one's intellectual credibility). And those who confidently peddle such 'hell-fire' scenarios, endeavoring to scare people into 'heaven,' tend to paint a very poor picture of the Trinity and can do lasting damage to those seeking forgiveness and wholeness. The

---

[6] See, for example, Isa 10:1-2.
[7] Rutledge, *The Crucifixion: Understanding the Death of Jesus Christ*, Eerdmans (2015), 132.

Bible strongly discourages speculation concerning the details of the eschaton; we are told it is a mystery that not even Jesus knows![8] But those churches that are too embarrassed to even mention eschatology are presenting only half of the biblical narrative; it has lost the *hope* of the gospel.[9] Moreover, it is a capitulation to modernity. Both extremes are unhealthy for the church and the world. And both are not being faithful to the fullness of *God's* mission, which is our calling and priority for right now.

Returning to the question of relevance, if we scratch at the surface of our lives we will find that we harbor stress, anxiety, fear, regret, bitterness, resentment, angst, and a range of other negative emotions and attitudes that hold us in captivity. We are not always as free as we wish we were on the treadmill of life. It is perhaps no surprise then that our society is the most medicated in the world for depression, mental illness, and the like. Part of the problem is broken relationships and a fractured community and/or family life. We were created for wholesome relationships; a sense of interconnectedness rather than isolated individualism. As the English poet and cleric John Donne (1572-1631) famously said:

> *No man is an island entire of itself; every man is a piece of the continent, a part of the main . . . any man's death diminishes me, because I am*

---

[8] Mark 13; Matt 24; Luke 21. These chapters are certainly pertinent to the destruction of Jerusalem in 70 CE, but to restrict their interpretation just to that event is misleading in terms of the overall biblical narrative.
[9] See Wright, *Surprised by Hope: Rethinking Heaven, the Resurrection, and the Mission of the Church,* HarperOne (2008).

involved in mankind. And therefore never send to know for whom the bell tolls; it tolls for thee.[10]

Part of the remedy is to be in 'community,' a network of life-giving, loving relationships of mutual support and encouragement. But that is evidently not enough, because in addition to social brokenness there is a spiritual malaise. The Adam and Eve story tells us, "The LORD God said, 'It is not good that the man should be alone; I will make him a helper as his partner.'"[11] The intention for both was to be in an intimate relationship with their Maker. When we slow down from our frenetic pace of life long enough to listen in the silence to our deepest longings, the emptiness we sometimes feel is really a *spiritual* void. This is evidence of a deep, latent desire to be loved unconditionally—as we are by God. In St. Augustine's words, "You have made us for yourself, O Lord, and our heart is restless until it rests in you." We have a profound need for acceptance and forgiveness, not just to be a part of community, important though that is, but to know we are each a beloved child of God. Those whose lives have experienced brokenness, sadness, and powerlessness are more open to this message than are society's 'winners.' Mark tells us that Jesus said: "Those who are well have no need of a physician, but those who are sick; I have come to call not the righteous but sinners."[12] To those in bondage to all that distorts right relationships, Jesus said: "If the Son makes you

---

[10] Meditation XVII, in *Devotions upon Emergent Occasions*, published in 1624. Donne wrote this meditation on death when he was seriously ill in 1623.
[11] Gen 2:18
[12] Mark 2:17. See also Luke 5:32; 19:10; Matt 9:13.

free, you will be free indeed."[13] Christians believe Jesus' message of forgiveness, freedom, and acceptance lives on. John's conclusion to his gospel includes both a blessing on his followers and their Spirit-filled commissioning:

> *Jesus said to them again, "Peace be with you. As the Father has sent me, so I send you." When he had said this, he breathed on them and said to them, "Receive the Holy Spirit. If you forgive the sins of any, they are forgiven them; if you retain the sins of any, they are retained."*[14]

Jesus passes on his authority *to forgive sins* to his church. While the church has—at times—abused that authority in the past, nevertheless, our being sent into the world is not only to teach and baptize but to bring divine forgiveness.[15] That is a key element of being in community with the Trinity as we live out the reign of God together.

These responses to the question of relevance, then, address suffering, death, justice, hope, forgiveness, and unconditional love, and provide relational meaning and purpose to life in the context of *God's* narrative, not one of our own making. Those who are confident that Jesus is irrelevant must—presumably—already be assured of the alternatives, whether they are political, sociological, or philosophical. While the skeptic may have legitimate doubts as to the reality of the reign of God, I find uncritical confidence in the alternatives baffling.

---

[13] John 8:36
[14] John 20: 21-23
[15] Matt 28:18-20

The Lord Be With You

Finally, the traditional liturgy contains the well-known phrase, "The Lord be with you." This is both an affirmation and a declaration; we are called to be aware of God's promised *presence*. While God's Spirit can always surprise us, I suggest that you can only *expect* to experience God's presence if you actually believe God *is* relevant—not just in terms of the big issues mentioned above, but to everyday life. Perhaps, then, there is a direct correlation between losing confidence in the Jesus-story and a lack of awareness of God's presence. The quest for relevance leads us, in the end, to the nurturing of *faith*. This begins with believing that we truly matter to God, and that we are a part of a story that is much bigger than ourselves.

"The Lord Be With You"
Part Two: A Narrative of Presence
Tim Reddish

When I was just finishing my undergraduate degree in physics, I was wrestling with the issue of divine 'guidance.' My embedded theology at the time likened my Christian journey to traveling along predetermined train tracks, and I was being presented with a switch in the track with two possible career paths. Should I pursue a PhD in physics or should I accept a job offer designing reactors in the nuclear power industry? Which one did *God* want me to do? I prayerfully agonized over this choice as if there was only one right answer. The switch in the train track therefore presented a choice between one way which was 'God's will' and one which was not. I recall seeking

God in prayer and getting no definitive response to my question. It never occurred to me that my question presupposed various theological and philosophical assumptions, not least in terms of God's relationship with time and the notion of predestination! What was I to do? It was then that I believed that God said to me: "You choose!"

Given my rigid theological framework, this seemed a very strange response to my prayer request, yet I was at peace in thinking that this was indeed the voice of God's Spirit. And so I chose to work toward a PhD. Shortly after having made my decision, I remember thinking that this had been a profound spiritual learning experience. In this situation, there wasn't one correct path to follow. Both choices were equally good, and even if one has doubts about the ethics or morality of nuclear power (which one did in the early 1980s after the Three Mile Island incident), God still wants responsible people to work in this industry. In saying, "You choose," God was graciously informing me I had genuine freewill. In other words, not only would God respect my decision, he would be with me whatever I chose. That's quite a lesson!

In hindsight, I could articulate this scenario in a different way. The train-track analogy corresponds to a digital view of decision-making, or 'guidance;' the future is already known to God, hence one track would take me to the destination corresponding to 'God's will,' and the other would not. The underlying assumption—erroneously, and perhaps largely based on fear—is that being on the track *God* wants guarantees 'blessing'! In reality, this way of thinking is based on a desire for *certainty*, which is the opposite of journeying in *faith*.¹ I now believe in a very different, open view of God's guidance. It's more analog, rather than digital, and it involves knowing in your core being that *'God is with you'* as you journey toward the Light.

More recently, this notion of 'God being with you' was underscored most vividly when my first wife, Anne, was diagnosed with cancer. What I discovered along our journey of suffering is described extensively elsewhere.² Thankfully, we were well-supported by our minister, close friends, and our church. Naturally, we all prayed for complete healing as Anne underwent surgery, followed by chemotherapy and radiation treatment. Even so, we did not want to make any big 'claims' that Anne was healed. We were simply content to say, "God is with us," throughout. As long we knew Immanuel ("God with us") *deep within our core being* then, whatever happened, we would be alright. Of course we all certainly hoped and prayed for a miracle, but our faith in God was not dependent upon whether or not God healed Anne.

This attitude, it seems to me, corresponds well with the often-quoted verses: "Do not be anxious about anything, but in everything by prayer and supplication with thanksgiving let your requests be made known to God. And *the peace of God, which surpasses all understanding, will guard your hearts and your minds in Christ Jesus.*"³ I can honestly say that we did experience a profound sense of peace during our ordeal. But, I hastily

---

[1] See Heb 11:1 and 2 Cor 5:7
[2] See Reddish, *Does God Always Get What God Wants?*, Cascade (2018).
[3] Phil 4:6-8. See also John 14:27, where Jesus says, "Peace I leave with you; my peace I give to you. I do not give to you as the world gives [i.e., *pax romana*]. Do not let your hearts be troubled, and do not let them be afraid."

add, this is not a reflection on us but on God's *graciousness* towards us. Nor did this mean we were stoic, or did not experience times of anxiety, tears, grief, and sadness. We were human! But even in those times, we still knew God was with us.[4] That deep peace and the fact that it "surpasses all understanding" shows that there is an *irrational* element to having such peace of mind, especially in our circumstances.

But the story does not end there, as Anne's cancer later returned and spread. What does it mean, in terms of the conversation with God that we call prayer, when that happens? This topic is too vast to address here, either theologically or pastorally, but don't misconstrue brevity (or inadequate nuance) as being indicative of insufficient wrestling with the complex issue of suffering. We lived with this for six years; that's ample time to read and reflect! My conclusions might surprise some Christians.

First, it is always appropriate to continue asking God for healing, because it's always right to ask! But, when Anne's cancer *spread*, we acknowledged that the signs increasingly pointed to the fact that God was unlikely to heal her and even that she might not live for much longer. When the situation became 'terminal,' as it eventually did, our faith cannot be a denial of that fact. That would be inauthentic. After all, we believe that God will not abandon us *even in death*, don't we?[5]

Second, I calmly pondered the following question: "What if God *couldn't* heal Anne? What if God was doing all that he could—allowing us to feel his presence, extending Anne's life, sparing her from excessive

---

[4] I confess I have not always had such peace in other areas of my life!
[5] See Rom 8:38-39

suffering, providing quality of life, giving us peace that passes understanding, never leaving us alone—but, in this specific situation, God could not heal Anne?"

This question was asked *not* in 'unfaith,' but in light of a *faith-filled* community's persistent prayer… and the reality of the disease continuing to metastasize. I had no doubt that a loving God would *want* Anne to experience healing and wholeness, so it was not that God *wouldn't* heal Anne. To question that is to doubt the *character* of God as revealed in Jesus, regardless as to how one understands the nature of divine attributes.

Christians who recoil at the notion of 'God *cannot*…' do so because they are firmly committed to the classical view of divine omnipotence, which, put crudely, implies God can do *anything*. When this attribute is linked with God's omniscience and then wrapped in divine transcendence, we end up with a God who is in absolute 'control,' a micromanager. Hence, since God *didn't* heal Anne, God must *not* have *wanted* to heal Anne. Wow, that's quite an assertion about God's character!

I recently was driving along the road and saw a Church sign: "God is in control, so you have nothing to fear." Is this the kind of control envisaged? When I look at the dark side of our earthly experience—of human wickedness, mindless evil, and the untamed power of nature, all of which can have disastrous, far-reaching consequences—and think that God might 'control' all of this, it really *does* fill me with fear. Such a capricious God does not inspire love, devotion, or praise. No wonder we have atheists if that is what Christians profess!

This view of God's activity within creation is connected with a Greek notion of the divine. It does not begin with the relational Trinity or with the heart of God that is revealed in the teachings and actions of Jesus. What we see in the gospel accounts is that God does not *want* people to suffer or to be in bondage of any kind. That being the case, if we persist in seeking a response to the "why?" question, we must focus our attentions elsewhere. Instead of placing the absence of overt healing in the realm of 'lack of faith,' or in God's character, I believe we must explore the subtle nature of divine action—God's continuing relationship with creation. Amongst other things, this means considering what God *can* and *cannot* do and differentiating that from what God *wants* and *does not want* to do (or to be done by us who partner with God to further his kingdom).

Rather than emphasizing, "God is in control," how about focusing on, "God is here"?

The theme of divine presence runs throughout the Old Testament narrative.[6] At times the psalmists anguished over God's apparent silence or absence, and they even wondered whether God had abandoned his covenant people. Job had the same dilemma. Israel's ultimate sense of forsakenness was experienced in the Babylonian Exile. We must not, however, naïvely expect that God's presence is to be experienced at the same intensity at all times. We are inclined to think this way when we say that God is omnipresent. The writers of the Old Testament appreciated

---

[6] See Terrence E. Fretheim, *The Suffering Of God*, (Philadelphia, Fortress, 1984), 60-78.

that God's vivid presence in theophany (Moses and the burning bush, whirlwinds, clouds, etc.) was most unusual. Moreover, God's presence was understood to be centered upon the Ark of the Covenant in the Tabernacle and, later, the Temple.[7] So God's continual presence was understood to have intensifications at certain times and places, just like our experiences of being 'in love.'

Now, with that backdrop, consider the notion of divine presence in the New Testament. Jesus, in the words of the Great Commission, says: "All authority in heaven and on earth has been given to me… and remember, *I am with you always, to the end of the age*."[8] Jesus also promises the fearful and confused disciples that the Holy Spirit will *abide in* them.[9] Luke portrays a radical change in the Jewish understanding of divine presence at Pentecost, and Peter explains the coming of the Spirit to the common person (as opposed to kings and prophets) as a fulfillment of Joel's prophecy.[10] All this, and more, provides a basis for *expecting* God to be with us as we journey onward in faith.

In a pastoral context, the experiential reality of 'God being here' is often referred to as a 'ministry of presence.' This should *not* be viewed as minimalistic, in the sense that God's activity in the world is reduced to merely being manifest through individuals. Such a restricted portrayal of pastoral care is a betrayal of the theological richness associated with the

---

[7] This is one reason why the destruction of the Temple in Jerusalem was so devastating.
[8] Matt 28:18-20
[9] John 14: 16-18; see also 20: 21-22
[10] See Acts 2

kingdom of God. It represents a lack of faith that God genuinely acts in history, even if we are not quite sure how to articulate precisely *how* God does act within his creation! What we call miracles can—and do—happen. Therefore it is right to pray boldly for them. Nevertheless, a pastoral team's role in dealing with grieving and hurting parishioners is to vividly *re-present* Jesus to them in their situations. Coming alongside someone in their suffering, and listening and walking with them, is crucial. This is the horizontal aspect of community, but it must also invoke the vertical dimension of communion with a suffering Trinitarian God who experienced the full horrors of the cross.

What I have alluded to above is that it is vitally important for *sufferers* to recognize *for themselves* the presence of God in those who walk with them on their journey—including medical professionals. But it must go a step further, namely, an awareness of God's Spirit being *within them* as they experience their own dark nights of the soul. Caregivers cannot be there all of the time, so the experience of the profound—even mystical—sense of peace in those alone times is essential, and is a testament to the presence of a covenantal God. Praying with expectation for a heightened intensification or awareness of God's presence is definitely appropriate in times of suffering. I can certainly say that Anne and I experienced God's presence—yes, with variations in intensity—on our six-year journey together with cancer, which sadly ended with her dying on January 30th 2011.

Without such peace, there is, understandably, a tendency to be fearful in the face of medical reality. But even in that reality, the Christian has grounds for *hope*—not in clinging to the fading hope of a last-minute miracle, but confidence in the resurrected Jesus Christ who walks alongside us. Jesus walked-the-walk *and* talked-the-talk. He carried his own cross, even collapsing under its weight and needing help, as he walked toward his slow and painful death. Our hope arises from the resurrection, without which our faith is meaningless.[11] Jesus, who walks with us personally, knows the route of suffering, and he also knows that death is not the last word.

Since Anne's death, I have left my successful physics career in academia and studied theology at seminary. I am now happily remarried to a wonderful woman named Mary. This is another indication that God is continually at work bringing good out of evil. I have recently been ordained as a minister and become a pastor. All my life experiences come with me into this exciting new phase of my life. And I am also aware that God continues to be with me on this adventure of faith.

"The Lord be with *you*."

Rev. Dr. Tim Reddish, a former physics professor,
is the minister at St Andrews Presbyterian Church in Amherstburg, Ontario.
asamatteroffaith.com

---

[11] See 1 Cor. 15

Why Does Narrative Matter

Why does narrative matter? Well, to begin with, people have been telling stories since the dawn of time. In fact,

History is nothing but a series of stories that, **when told correctly**, *can teach us lessons, give us insights into a variety of concepts, or entertain us. Every story serves a purpose, even if to simply relay a message. Without history, without chronicled stories, mankind would never learn from his mistakes, would never dream to emulate past heroes, would never see anything but the now. We would be clueless to the past, and therefore helpless for the future.*[1]

---

[1] Big Fish Presentations. "A Very Brief History of Storytelling." 28 Feb. 2012, https://bigfishpresentations.com/2012/02/28/a-very-brief-history-of-storytelling/ (emphasis mine).

Please don't miss what I find to be the most important phrase in this quote..."*when told correctly.*" The stories we tell (and the languages we use) have certainly evolved over time, from oral traditions… to semi-permanent cave paintings and stone carvings… to the printed word… to television and movies… to the snippets of life we share on social media in an ever changing, sometimes moment by moment account. But in all of these ways, we have narratives told correctly and incorrectly.

In some things there is a recognition of this disparity. As an example, the social media 'you' probably displays your 'highlight reel' (unless you're one of those people who really loves to air your dirty laundry in public). There's this sort of understanding that explicitly public interactions are made for celebrations or sympathy, but we don't generally share the complete history of our personal lives and heritage in images attached to 25 word blurbs.

The real problem comes in when we have entire histories of real people which have been deleted (or at the very least significantly censored) in the sources we regard as credible. Research based in the study of personal accounts of marginalized people groups (in written and interview formats) has led me to an intriguing common thread. Regardless of the bias which creates marginalization, many of these narratives are described as 'lost,' allowing the identity of whole people groups to be threatened and damaged, seemingly in the name of comfort and security for oppressors. Something is terribly wrong with that.

Conclusion: Why Does Narrative Matter

We live in an age of media saturation, where very fine lines exists between exploiting the narratives of the other and serving as advocates, and between serving as advocates and empowering others to share on *their* terms. Usurping the experience of another, in order to advance an agenda, is not redemptive, even if we intended it to be so. It is fascinating how we conflate words like enable and empower. At our best, we attempt to tell the good stories of people who have overcome impediments of some sort to look, feel, and act just like we do. But, these 'good' stories are shared from an outside perspective, and so even they must be vetted and tempered. Drawing on the experience of exile, Edward W. Said issues this cautionary statement which relates directly to all kinds of suffering and trauma:

> *Exile is strangely compelling to think about but terrible to experience. It is the unhealable rift forced between a human being and a native place, between the self and its true home: its essential sadness can never be surmounted. And while it is true that literature and history contain heroic, romantic, glorious, even triumphant episodes in an exile's life, these are no more than efforts meant to overcome the crippling sorrow of estrangement. The achievements of exile are permanently undermined by the loss of something left behind forever.*[2]

In our typical selective storytelling, we may easily mistake verified written accounts of history for a comprehensive body of memory and

---

[2] Said, Edward W. *Reflections on Exile: and Other Essays*. Harvard University Press: Cambridge, MA, 2002, 173.

experience, but these are not the same thing. And so, in addition to our desire to be the kind of people who step in and save the day (most often in the only ways we know how, whether those are contextually appropriate or not), we should also recognize the need for stories to be shared as firsthand accounts, whenever possible, and at the very least as accounts coming from people who are close to the unfolding narrative as opposed to simply reporting about it. This is sometimes easier said than done. As I alluded to in the introduction, it can be immensely difficult to share personal narratives, because they are exactly that—personal. Within the confines of these experiences, we feel joy and sorrow, pleasure and pain, overwhelming love and consuming numbness. It is all part of being human, and it can be too much to expose publicly. Undoubtedly, it is easier to tell the story of someone else, to write pseudonymously, or to engage in endless banter about theories and philosophies of theodicy without any easily recognizable skin in the game. This leads me to a brief, and certainly incomplete, exploration of why stories are sometimes left untold.

How Do Narratives Get Lost... and Found

We live in an era when people are bravely coming forward with their stories of life and love and oppression and pain, so it may seem odd to place so much concern on the idea that many narratives *have* been lost. One might ask, aren't they actually being found at break-neck speed? Although it is good that more and more spaces for safe dialogue are

Conclusion: Why Does Narrative Matter

emerging, there are still so many things left unsaid. Three reasons stand out to me, above others:

    First, some narratives are lost because there is no longer a firsthand account, and the story was never passed down. These are difficult stories to grieve, particularly if there is some external factor which forces us to know the story was, indeed, real, and even more so if we assume an unbearable degree of suffering within its lost-ness. An example might be the experience of a person who dies alone. Since no one witnessed the death, there is no way to recover what happened. One might be able to recover some level of *fact* based on forensic evidence, one might be able to deduce the surrounding circumstances, which may either comfort or distress the living, but one can never fully claim the part of this history that is the sensory perception or reactions of the affected person. Those feelings, movements, and words are forever undisclosed. "There is a difference between the narration of historical facts by just anyone and the narration of history by those who have lived through it."[3] This may be an appropriate loss of narrative in specific and unique situations in that we are not culpable for what cannot be known. Interestingly, on an open theology view, there is a God who knows, because even if one holds to the idea that God does not definitively know the future (although many open theists believe God knows each and every possibility); I have yet to encounter any theist who does not believe God knows every detail of the past. Willie James Jennings puts this into words

---

[3] Oliver, Kelly. Witnessing: Beyond Recognition. University of Minnesota Press, Minneapolis, MN, 2001, 85.

which are eloquent and profound, bringing a sense of presence and healing when he writes,

> *God remembers what others have forgotten. The peoples destroyed by evil, the cries of anguish and pain, the injustice covered over and long forgotten, the hidden truths, the inside stories, the complexities of agency that meant that the action done was not the action intended, the man, woman, and child who each died alone and forgotten—all these things and more God remembers. The animals that no one knew, the trees that no human eyes ever saw, the bugs that flourished only in the sight of God —all these things and more God remembers. The plans, ideas, hopes, dreams, songs, poems, dances, touches, and smiles that escaped all the practices that enable us to remember, God remembers this—and more.[4]*

In this sense, nothing is ever completely lost, although it may be lost to our human capability to remember.

Second, some stories are lost because people in power want it to be this way. Joined to the concern about missing chapters and books and volumes of history is this idea that history must be viewed from a particular view only, and that (of course) is most often the dominant view. But "vigilance is necessary to avoid the reduction of history to its evidence and facts."[5] A great discrepancy between facts and truth may

---

[4] Jennings, Willie James. "War Bodies: Remembering Bodies in a Time of War." *POST-TRAUMATIC PUBLIC THEOLOGY*, edited by Stephanie N. Arel and Shelly Rambo, PALGRAVE MACMILLAN, 2016, pp. 23–35.
[5] Oliver, 142.

Conclusion: Why Does Narrative Matter

exist. We can spin a story to *mean* just about anything, if we try hard enough and have the resources to be convincing. This is *not* an acceptable reason for lost narrative, and it calls for some extraordinary courage on the part of those whose histories have been oppressed and marginalized in order to make a dent in the prevailing approach to historical accounts. Related to this, some stories are lost because humanity, as a whole, has not always believed the stories people have told. This is also a reason widely cited by victims for why they have never told their stories or have taken years to do so. We've most recently seen this on both sides of the coin with the #MeToo movement and the many charges of abuse and assault that have surfaced. Experience, both personal and collective, plays an enormous role in our theology and our systems of morals and values. To blanketly discredit the narratives of others is to essentially tell them they do not exist as human beings in the world who have had particular experiences. Do people lie? Yes, sometimes. This is a risk of human interaction, but if we enter into every conversation with an assumption of dishonesty as the baseline, the stories will be dismissed out of hand, discredited, and covered up, *or* people will simply stop telling them in order to protect themselves from further injury. Either way, the stories and the truth therein are unjustifiably lost.

Third... and this one is tricky... Some stories are lost, because the participants of the narrative have determined for one reason or another that it is best for them to remain silent. The current cultural context of which I am a part does not allow for this, if respect is to be had. Even though I am a major proponent of story sharing and truth telling, I do think we need to reassess our insistence that people *always* share their most intense suffering, because although the push for this kind of candor has been healing for many, it is also harmful for some. Suffering people deserve the time and space they need to grieve appropriately, as defined by themselves, whether that lines up with 'typical' timelines or lasts a lifetime. As good listeners, we owe it to our fellow humans to trust their judgment in regard to the sharing of their own narratives. There are, therefore, appropriate times during which to let go of the story while corporately lamenting the suffering even without knowing the details. Silence (although never silencing) is sometimes a suitable response, embodying availability and presence.

So, What About the Specific Stories in this Book?

This work clearly focuses on the second kind of endangered narrative, for these are raw, real, personal stories that people chose freely to share. I have occasionally been accused of vomiting my feelings all over my writing (perhaps just venting), and I know there is some truth in this charge. But, I also feel passionately about the value of giving away my platforms in order to allow others the safe space to speak into my life and into the lives of all who will listen. Yet there's something more. This kind of engagement moves beyond listening to witnessing.

The language of witness and testimony is, itself, deeply rooted within Christian culture. It denotes a sharing of experiential truth and encompasses both the teller and the hearer, but Christianity does not have

Conclusion: Why Does Narrative Matter

a corner on witnessing, and we all have so much to learn from one another. Jewish literary critic Shoshana Felman writes, witnessing:

> *identifies the uniqueness of eye-witness testimony in the performance of testimony, which goes beyond the firsthand knowledge of the witness. The performance of testimony says more than the witness knows. And only the supplement of this more than knowledge can speak the truth of experience, a truth repeated and yet constituted in the very act of testimony.*[6]

Those of us who witness to another's story can do so only in a second-hand type of testimony, because words are not enough to fully engage the truth of history. We do not always have a sympathetic understanding of what our neighbors, near and far away, are suffering, but if we believe in a God who both affects and is affected, due to God's entangled embodiment with humanity and the world, as a whole; we do have a responsibility to act as people created in the image of Love. The now famous words of Fred Rogers call us to response and responsibility among the suffering. He said, "When I was a boy and I would see scary things in the news, my mother would say to me, 'Look for the helpers. You will always find people who are helping.'"[7]

It's not difficult to find ways to encounter this kind of pain, and although it is sometimes overwhelming (no one person can do *everything*), it is also within our reach to do *something* about it, as helpers. Acting as

---

[6] Oliver, 85-86.
[7] Widely attributed to Fred Rogers, perhaps first published in a newspaper column in the 1980s.

agents of redemption in the world is our highest calling. There is not one right answer for what this looks like, but there are basic principles that allow us to move forward, in hope, be it ever so tenuous. One of these is dialogue. I feel so privileged to have been granted permission to share the stories of these friends of mine, first because it is important for their stories to be heard, but also because it is vital to engage in continued conversation surrounding the very real suffering in the world, which touches us all in some way.

Several themes emerged in the compilation of these essays. Unsurprisingly, childhood trauma was among the most often reported suffering encountered as these pieces began to fill my inbox. In the first three essays, Greene, Karris, and McConnaughey take us on journeys that are both heartrending and hopeful, as they relate their own stories of personal, family, and communal development, told in ways that emphasize the effects of traumatic experience on children who need loving guidance from the people they trust most to make sense of the world. This matters deeply for theological development, as our views about God are most easily shaped during our formative childhood years. One thing that stood out prominently to me is the profound ability of children to understand who God is. Greene's delightful story connecting nature and his early experience of God's presence within him (in his very belly) is tempered by the sometimes helpful yet sometimes confusing ways in which the church shapes theology. Of course, all of us are subject to some necessary deconstruction of inaccurate theology (wouldn't it be fabulous if we could just get it all 'right' the first time… or ever…), but this goes hand in hand

Conclusion: Why Does Narrative Matter

with the beautiful presence of church communities who came alongside each of these authors to help them reconstruct a healthier view of God, the church, and community. It's never neatly wrapped with a bow, but there are, indeed, things that can be done and relationships that can be forged, which incite healing and growth in the process of living.

But what about when the church plays a role in the suffering? What about when the church acts as the oppressor? I cannot begin to recount the number of times I have heard horror stories about the exclusivity and damnation that often takes place within the walls of the very place where we should be most welcomed into community, created Imago Dei, as the people of God. Harvey's essay shares some insightful truths about the tension and messiness that accompanies church life and calling when personal history does not line up perfectly with expectations. Krabbe answers (not directly, but prophetically), challenging the church to open so wide its doors that even those who are far beyond the typical expectations might find a place to not only belong but to effectively minister to one another. Rather than the often restrictive nature of worthiness and voice; presence and priesthood are opened to all, demanding greater (not less) responsibility and accountability as the church struggles to identify what it is to be the people of God, following the pattern of Jesus. Through this type of thinking, a healthier, more robust theology begins to take shape: If this inclusivity of loving presence is how we understand God, then how should we act accordingly?

This segues well into another theme that emerged, including narratives of identity and agency which required vulnerability and risk when communicating with other human beings. If we really believe what we preach, how might we practice this inclusivity in daily rhythms in our homes and relationships? It's easy to give lip service to the idea that God loves everybody when everyone around us looks the same. But how do we respond when relationships are confronted with, or even broken by, tensions that shake the very core of who we are? The short pieces by Breningstall-Ismael, Elias, and Graham appeal to deeply personal engagements which call into question our reactions to, and interactions with, those who possess different core commitments. These three essays do not fit neatly with the rest of the book, and, in fact, I wondered if their presence might irreparably rupture the coherency therein. Then I decided it didn't much matter if they do, because that is exactly the point! In embracing an uncontrolling, self-emptying God who is love, we relinquish our right to walk away from those whose presence shakes our perceived stability and challenges our position.

To love is to act, and we cannot act if we are not present. Also, my favorite line in this entire body of work comes from the Breningstall-Ismael piece, "I truly thought facts and love would be enough." There was no way I was leaving that out, particularly because of the weighty and timely reminder that follows: there are certainly people for whom these things are not enough, but it's not most people. Hope still resounds loudly.

Last, come the stories of the anxiety and grief that accompany physical ailments and death. These are interesting, because they do not

Conclusion: Why Does Narrative Matter

correspond directly with the basic definition of trauma, which is more event oriented than ongoing. It has caused me to consider the false dichotomy we often draw in religious (and specifically Christian) language between salvific crisis moments and the daily process of becoming who we are created to be. In the essays by Rich, Sweeney, Reddish, and myself, we read about difficult, ongoing experiences that manifest first as physical but that also affect human bodies in a holistic manner which creates the potential for integration into a new normal but one that remains traumatic in its configuration and thus requires continued transformation and processing over a long time span. It is difficult enough to integrate traumatic moments, so what of traumatic years or decades? Something that caught my attention within these narratives (and perhaps this is especially so, since my own is included) was the recognition of the participants that they are telling what seems like the same story over and over again, so new audiences become necessary. This has caused me to question our patience (or lack thereof) with the healing process.

Where Do We Go From Here

Undoubtedly, I live in a pragmatically structured culture with an almost innate 'fix it or get over it,' mentality. Those experiencing trauma and suffering do not respond well to these conditions, nor should they, but how might we best respond and integrate in such a way that we do not encourage cycles of perpetual crisis or abuse? This is an age old question for those who care deeply.

The temptation remains to gloss over radical suffering in such a way that God takes on all of the responsibility and culpability, and we do not. After all, if we *can* comfort others with platitudes and clichés, why not take the easy way out? The answer is: This is not responsible theology or empathetic human behavior! Melissa Raphael uses ancient wisdom to shed new light on this very issue when she writes, "There is an old and fragile narrative running through the tradition of a God whose heart will break if *we* do not *mend*..."[8] These words serve as a double entendre (although I am unsure whether this was Raphael's intent or not).

God is so intricately intertwined with humanity that God's heart breaks when we are broken, ourselves, *and* when we do not work toward the healing of others. We must mend and mend. This requires community. In an attempt to fix instead of heal, in our zeal, we often rush ahead to activism without action. The intent is right, but the follow-through is lacking, if we do not first sit with the pain and suffering—listening intently to the expressed needs of the other to share space together and bring validity to the ongoing narrative. This requires testimony and witness. Much like God is ever present and always doing everything God can do to redeem the world, we are called to partner with God in these same ways, first simply being in relationship and only then acting as we are able. It is time consuming work, and the results are almost never quick or complete, but they are good and progressive.

---

[8] Raphael, Melissa. "Wrestling With God: Jewish Responses During and After the Holocaust." Oxford University Press: USA, 654.

Conclusion: Why Does Narrative Matter

A Challenge to Share

And so there emerges a challenge for all of us to share. Perhaps ironically, it is one of the first things we attempt to teach children when they realize they are not the only living beings in the world, and yet it continues to be a lifelong struggle. This challenge takes two forms, for sharing is an act of both giving and receiving. Listening is integral to the work of healing, but without telling there is no listening. In order to fully share in this dialogic exchange, we must sometimes play the role of the listener and sometimes play the role of the speaker, while always playing the role of an interpreter of the interplay between language and silences.

The competitive nature of suffering, which labels some pain as greater and more worthy of exploration has created a tension in which it can sometimes be tempting to think you do not have a story that counts if you haven't experienced namable horrors such as poverty, war, discrimination, abuse, or the like, but I would like to encourage you to share your experience anyway, because you may find common ground and similarities with others than can lead to greater understanding of emotional affects if not parallel experience. The goal is not to seek out the worst story among us but the ways in which we might dignify one another's humanity, through love. Each person deserves this, whether the lost narratives that surface are unbearable in nature or correspond with a more typical sense of loss, which we have all experienced at some point in time.

Vulnerability is hard. Testimony is hard. Listening is hard. But, just about everything worthwhile in life is hard, so find your people and share your stories anyway! As you do, try not to lose sight of the value of narrative for narrative's sake and for furthering historical accuracy and truth telling, but also consider some questions that might guide your actions moving forward into the new reality of life after suffering.

These might include:

- How has your perception of theology (the study of God) changed in light of your experiences of suffering and trauma?
- How have your faith traditions (or lack thereof) played positive or negative roles in the sharing and healing process?
- What old practices (naming clichés, minimizing suffering, blaming God, etc.) are you ready to let go in order to engage more fully in partnership with God and others toward redemption and healing?
- What new practices (testimony, witness, etc.) are you ready to take up as you live into vulnerability and community building?
- What common issues are emerging in your telling and listening that might strengthen empathetic relationships and greater understanding of your fellow human beings?
- How might you encourage the people in your current contexts and communities to engage in more sharing and listening practices?

Conclusion: Why Does Narrative Matter

Thank you so much for taking the time to read this book and to genuinely consider why and how experience and personal narrative shape theology. Although it may be debatable in some circles, I come from a Wesleyan tradition which bases much of our theological inquiry on a quadrilateral encompassing tradition, reason, and experience as theological foundations on which to stand, ultimately filtered through the lens of Scripture. On that view, experience has always been essential to our understanding of God and God's relationship to humanity and the world. In essence, this means our lives weaved together in all of their mundane, joyful, and sorrowful moments matter deeply in our understanding of who God is and who we are. Experience can never be the only factor in our developing theology, but it must play a major role, for our practice defines our faith as much as our faith determines our practice. And if one chooses to believe in an indeterminate future in which God knows every possibility but we are still responsible to make choices to determine and fulfill these possibilities, then the stakes are high. So go forth and live into the story of you, fundamentally connected to the greater story of us and the ultimate story of Love.

www.ingramcontent.com/pod-product-compliance
Lightning Source LLC
Chambersburg PA
CBHW031257110426
42743CB00040B/711